TREE OF LIFE

a book of wisdom for men

TREE OF LIFE

a book of wisdom for men

BIBLICAL WISDOM
FOR EVERYDAY LIVING
Selected by Eric Kampmann

BEAUFORT BOOKS
NEW YORK

To Anne

"A wife of noble character"

—Proverbs 31:10

ACKNOWLEDGMENTS

Beyond the Bible itself, no writing has had a greater influence on the direction of my life than the Christian classic, *My Utmost For His Highest* by Oswald Chambers. Chambers' life, his ministry and his death remain an extraordinary story to this day. Chambers died at the young age of 42 while serving the Lord and the British troops in the Egyptian desert in the twilight of the Great War. In the ordinary course of human affairs the world would not have noted the passing of this great and humble Christian teacher, but through the heroic perseverance of his wife, Biddy, a small portion of his writings were published as a devotional many years later. Ever since, Oswald Chambers' loving, vibrant and powerful influence has touched the lives of millions. He has certainly touched mine.

If we could account for all the people who have had an influence on the direction of our lives, we would be overwhelmed. The numbers are inexhaustible and would fill a book of their own. But I would like to thank a few people who have played a direct role in development and publication of *Tree Of Life*. First, I want to thank my irrepressible mother. Her optimism is indestructible. I want to thank my brothers, David and Steven and my sister, Megan, as well as their families. I want to acknowledge my own sons, Alex, Peter and Arthur, who prompted the idea for this book. And I must mention my beautiful daughter, Elizabeth, who likes to read the daily passages together with me. And while I have dedicated the book to her, I would like to thank my wife who has been a greater influence on the positive direction of my life than she will ever know.

There are many who have played a direct role in the publication of this book, but I would like to mention a few who have contributed above and beyond. First, to my wonderful partners, Gail Kump and Chris Bell; to Julie Hardison, Margaret Queen and Susan Hayes for being so good at what they do; to Janice Benight for her brilliant design and to Maryglenn Warnock for managing the publication of *Tree of Life* from beginning to end with humor and insight. Finally, and above all, I want to give praise and glory to my Lord and Savior Jesus Christ whose hand guided me through very troubled waters and led me on to higher and safer ground.

INTRODUCTION

"Taste and see
that the Lord is good;
Blessed is the man
who takes refuge in Him."
—PSALM 34:8

When things are going well, when times are prosperous and worries are few, it's easy to feel that we are in control. We attribute success to our own talents and abilities and build our lives on the premise of self-reliance. We spend our day-to-day life pursuing success and striving to meet a set of goals. There is nothing to stop us, unless, of course, one of life's harsh realities unexpectedly intrudes. If prosperity vanishes or good health disappears, then where do we turn for strength and support? If in better times we say, "leave me alone God, I have no time for you right now," then what do we say when we feel a desperate need to call on God for help? This dilemma is not new; every generation, in one way or another, declares its independence from God. Three thousand years ago, Job uttered words that sound familiar today: "Yet (we) say to God, 'leave us alone! We have no desire to know your ways. Who is the Almighty, that we should serve him? What would we gain by praying to him?'" (JOB 21:14–15)

Once, not long ago, my life was built on the soft foundation of self-reliance. I didn't actively reject God or deny His existence, but I was much too busy and career-driven to even consider the possibility of His having a role in my life. I attempted to live in a

God-free zone. But on the road to success and material well being, I ran into a reversal that almost destroyed everything I had built and nearly destroyed me as well. In 1989, I found myself facing bankruptcy, threats of lawsuits and financial devastation. With blinding speed my self-confidence was blown away and I was rendered vulnerable and defenseless. Fear filled every corner of my life. But when the chips were down and there was absolutely nowhere to turn, I cried out to God in my distress . . . and He answered!

His answer became clear to me only later. At the time, the situation was too chaotic for me to have any perspective. But in retrospect, I now realize that God saved me from those circumstances. When I look back on that bleak situation, I am reminded of a story in Daniel in which three men—Shadrach, Meshach and Abednego — are cast into a fire by order of King Nebuchadnezzar. The three men should have been consumed by the fire, yet they survived. I should have been consumed by my financial disaster, but I was not. I had experienced a miracle and I was amazed and over-whelmed. From that time on — first slowly, then with accelerating momentum — I turned away from a life built on self-reliance and instead acknowledged that my salvation came from God. I began to feel an enormous sense of gratitude and peace of mind.

After some of the wreckage had cleared, God spoke to my heart. This did not come to me in precise words; rather, it came upon me as a compelling need to come to know God better. It was as if He said, "I now want you to come to know me through my word and I want you to start now, not tomorrow." For a person in my state of complete Biblical ignorance, this was a staggering command. I had purchased a beautiful Bible in 1987, but like some giant obstacle, it seemed insurmountable and remained unopened and unused. Where would I begin? How could I come to understand what I was reading? And, furthermore, how would I find the time?

The answer came to me in the form of two simple words: "Start small." As I would later learn through my growing knowledge of the Bible, God loves the paradox of ordinary people doing mighty things on His behalf. Each of us is free to disregard God's voice, yet He always wants us to respond. I had a choice. I could turn away with any number of excuses or I could respond. And on February 13, 1991, I found a simple two-year reading plan that covers much of the Bible and I responded. I began to follow this plan and have followed it ever since. Through short selections, repetitive readings, Bible studies and church, my Biblical ignorance began to evaporate and in its place emerged an awareness of God's presence in my own life and in the world around me.

Whether it is a crisis or some other event that prompts a desire in you to come to know God, this book is designed as a starting place. The *Tree of Life* is an introduction to God's own word about life. The title comes from a reference to the tree of life found in Genesis and Revelation, the first and last books in the Bible. The book includes three hundred and sixty-six individual passages — one for each day of the calendar year — selected from six books in the Old Testament: Job, Psalms, Proverbs, Ecclesiastes, Song of Songs and Lamentations. Some of the passages are long, though never longer than a page. Some are short. Some passages are inspirational, while others are disturbing. Some verses are poetic and beautiful while some are practical and designed for everyday living. Most of the verses are over three thousand years old, yet each passage deals with issues that touch not only the lives of men today, but also generations and generations of men who have come before. For any man willing to listen, each verse will be startlingly fresh, relevant and true.

The *Tree of Life* was created as a way to share life-changing Biblical truths with men who may not be trained in Biblical scholarship or may not even have a working knowledge of the Old or New Testament. Also, I wanted to share the surprising benefits that come from systematic, daily readings in the Bible. By following such a system, I quickly reached a point where reading the Bible became an essential part of my everyday routine, no matter where I was or what I was doing. While this book is an introduction to systematic Biblical reading, it is my hope that you will take it much further and deeper with each succeeding year. If you read a passage from the *Tree of Life* every day and commit extra time for additional reading in the Bible and prayer, then, over a short period of time, you will set in place a routine that will become as important to you as anything you do. And at some point (for some sooner, for others later) you will become conversant in the language of the spirit of God.

The *Tree of Life* is a small first step, but it is a beginning. The concept of starting small is itself Biblical. Moses was appointed to speak to Pharaoh though he was "slow of speech and tongue." David was anointed by Samuel to be King though he was the least of Jesse's sons. Rahab was a prostitute, but she was part of God's plan for Israel and Jericho. Ruth, the great-grandmother of David, was not even an Israelite.

And Jesus, the Son of God, was born into extremely humble and dangerous circumstances. With God, it is wise to expect the unexpected.

As you come to know God's word through everyday reading, reflection and prayer, you will begin to feed the deep and abiding need in the human heart so eloquently expressed by Solomon in Ecclesiastes: "He has made everything beautiful in its time. He has also set eternity in the hearts of men . . ." (3:11). It is when our hearts open up to the reality of God's presence that we begin to experience the fullness and abundance that God always intended for us and we can say with the psalmist:

> *"Here I am, I have come—*
> *it is written about me in the scroll.*
> *I desire to do your will, O my God;*
> *your law is within my heart."*
> —PSALM 40:8

It is through the power of God's word that we learn the difference between a self-reliant life and a selfless life. We also gain what King Solomon called a "discerning heart" — the God-given ability to distinguish the important from the trivial. When God granted King Solomon anything he desired, King Solomon asked not for wealth, nor a long life, nor power over his enemies; instead, he asked God for a "discerning heart." The *Tree of Life* is offered to you as a useful, powerful and portable resource that can be used in all circumstances, not just during one of life's many emergencies. It is my prayer that God will grant each one of you a "discerning heart" and that reading in this book every day will open your life to the blessings that God wants for you.

PROLOGUE

And the LORD God said,
"The man has now become like one of us,
knowing good and evil.
He must not be allowed
to reach out his hand
and take also from the tree of life and eat,
and live forever."
So the LORD God banished him
from the Garden of Eden
to work the ground
from which he had been taken.
After he drove the man out,
he placed on the east side
of the Garden of Eden
cherubim and a flaming sword
flashing back and forth
to guard the way to the tree of life.

—FROM GENESIS 3:22–24

❧ A TREE OF LIFE

Blessed is the man who finds wisdom,
The man who gains understanding,
For she is more profitable than silver
And yields better returns than gold.
She is more precious than rubies;
Nothing you desire can compare with her.
Long life is in her right hand;
In her left hand are riches and honor.
Her ways are pleasant ways,
And all her paths are peace.
She is a tree of life to those who embrace her;
Those who lay hold of her will be blessed.

—PROVERBS 3:13-18

WONDERFULLY MADE

For you created my inmost being;
you knit me together in my mother's womb.
I praise you because I am fearfully and wonderfully made;
your works are wonderful,
I know that full well.
My frame was not hidden from you
when I was made in the secret place.
When I was woven together in the depths of the earth,
your eyes saw my unformed body.
All the days ordained for me
were written in your book
before one of them came to be.

—PSALM 139:13–16

HAVE YOU CONSIDERED MY SERVANT JOB?

One day the angels came to present themselves
before the LORD, and Satan also came with them.
The LORD said to Satan,
"Where have you come from?"
Satan answered the LORD,
"From roaming through the earth
and going back and forth in it."
Then the LORD said to Satan,
"Have you considered my servant Job?
There is no one on earth like him;
he is blameless and upright,
a man who fears God and shuns evil."

—JOB 1:6-8

Blessed Is the Man

Blessed is the man
who does not walk in the counsel of the wicked
or stand in the way of sinners
or sit in the seat of mockers.
But his delight is in the law of the Lord,
and on his law he meditates day and night.
He is like a tree planted by streams of water,
which yields its fruit in season
and whose leaf does not wither.
Whatever he does prospers.

—Psalm 1:1–3

❧ GET WISDOM, GET UNDERSTANDING

Listen, my sons, to a father's instruction;
pay attention and gain understanding.
I give you sound learning,
so do not forsake my teaching.
When I was a boy in my father's house,
still tender, and an only child of my mother,
he taught me and said,
"Lay hold of my words with all your heart;
keep my commands and you will live.
Get wisdom, get understanding;
do not forget my words or swerve from them.

—PROVERBS 4:1-5

CLEANSE ME FROM MY SIN

Have mercy on me, O God,
according to your unfailing love;
according to your great compassion
blot out my transgressions.
Wash away all my iniquity
and cleanse me from my sin.

For I know my transgressions,
and my sin is always before me.
Against you, you only, have I sinned
and done what is evil in your sight,
so that you are proved right when you speak
and justified when you judge.

Surely I was sinful at birth,
sinful from the time my mother conceived me.
Surely you desire truth in the inner parts;
you teach me wisdom in the inmost place.

—PSALM 51:1–6

WISDOM'S ORIGIN

"The LORD brought me forth as the first of his works,
before his deeds of old;
I was appointed from eternity,
from the beginning, before the world began.
When there were no oceans, I was given birth,
when there were no springs abounding with water;
before the mountains were settled in place,
before the hills, I was given birth,
before he made the earth or its fields
or any of the dust of the world.
I was there when he set the heavens in place,
when he marked out the horizon on the face of the deep,
when he established the clouds above
and fixed securely the fountains of the deep,
when he gave the sea its boundary
so the waters would not overstep his command,
and when he marked out the foundations of the earth.
Then I was the craftsman at his side.
I was filled with delight day after day,
rejoicing always in his presence,
rejoicing in his whole world
and delighting in mankind.

—PROVERBS 8:22-31

LIKE THE VENOM OF A SNAKE

Do you rulers indeed speak justly?
Do you judge uprightly among men?
No, in your heart you devise injustice,
and your hands mete out violence on the earth.
Even from birth the wicked go astray;
from the womb they are wayward and speak lies.
Their venom is like the venom of a snake,
like that of a cobra that has stopped its ears,
that will not heed the tune of the charmer,
however skillful the enchanter may be.

—PSALM 58:1–5

❧ THEY PLEAD FOR RELIEF

"Men cry out under a load of oppression;
they plead for relief from the arm the powerful.
But no one says, 'Where is God my Maker,
who gives songs in the night,
who teaches more to us than to the beasts of the earth
and makes us wiser than the birds of the air?'

—JOB 35:9-11

WHO MAY LIVE ON YOUR HOLY HILL?

LORD, who may dwell in your sanctuary?
Who may live on your holy hill?
He whose walk is blameless
and who does what is righteous,
who speaks the truth from his heart
and has no slander on his tongue,
who does his neighbor no wrong
and casts no slur on his fellowman,
who despises a vile man
but honors those who fear the Lord,
who keeps his oath even when it hurts,
who lends his money without usury
and does not accept a bribe against the innocent.

—PSALM 15:1–5

❧ MY SERVANT JOB

Then the LORD said to Satan,
"Have you considered my servant Job?
There is no one on earth like him;
he is blameless and upright,
a man who fears God and shuns evil.
And he still maintains his integrity,
though you incited me against him
to ruin him without any reason."

—JOB 2:3

A Burden Too Heavy to Bear

O Lord, do not rebuke me in your anger
or discipline me in your wrath.
For your arrows have pierced me,
and your hand has come down upon me.
Because of your wrath there is no health in my body;
my bones have no soundness because of my sin.
My guilt has overwhelmed me
like a burden too heavy to bear.

—PSALM 38:1–4

❧ LIKE A HIRED MAN

"Man born of woman
is of few days and full of trouble.
He springs up like a flower and withers away;
like a fleeting shadow, he does not endure.
Do you fix your eye on such a one?
Will you bring him before you for judgment?
Who can bring what is pure from the impure?
No one!
Man's days are determined;
you have decreed the number of his months
and have set limits he cannot exceed.
So look away from him and let him alone,
till he has put in his time like a hired man.

—JOB 14:1-6

January 14

❧ THEIR CHILDREN'S CHILDREN

As a father has compassion on his children,
so the LORD has compassion on those who fear him;
for he knows how we are formed,
he remembers that we are dust.
As for man, his days are like grass,
he flourishes like a flower of the field;
the wind blows over it and it is gone,
and its place remembers it no more.
But from everlasting to everlasting
the LORD's love is with those who fear him,
and his righteousness with their children's children—
with those who keep his covenant
and remember to obey his precepts.

—PSALM 103:13–18

❧ THERE WILL IT LIE

If clouds are full of water,
they pour rain upon the earth.
Whether a tree falls to the south or to the north,
in the place where it falls, there will it lie.
Whoever watches the wind will not plant;
whoever looks at the clouds will not reap.

—ECCLESIASTES 11:3-4

WHO IS LIKE YOU?

The heavens praise your wonders, O LORD,
your faithfulness too, in the assembly of the holy ones.
For who in the skies above can compare with the LORD?
Who is like the LORD among the heavenly beings?
In the council of the holy ones God is greatly feared;
he is more awesome than all who surround him.
O LORD God Almighty, who is like you?
You are mighty, O LORD,
and your faithfulness surrounds you.

—PSALM 89:5–8

❧ A GRIEVOUS EVIL

I have seen a grievous evil under the sun:
wealth hoarded to the harm of its owner,
or wealth lost through some misfortune,
so that when he has a son
there is nothing left for him.
Naked a man comes from his mother's womb,
and as he comes, so he departs.
He takes nothing from his labor
that he can carry in his hand.

—ECCLESIASTES 5:13-15

WHY ARE YOU DOWNCAST?

Why are you downcast, O my soul?
Why so disturbed within me?
Put your hope in God,
for I will yet praise him,
my Savior and my God.
My soul is downcast within me;
therefore I will remember you
from the land of the Jordan,
the heights of Hermon—from Mount Mizar.
Deep calls to deep
in the roar of your waterfalls;
all your waves and breakers
have swept over me.

—PSALM 42:5–7

HIS NAME ALONE IS EXALTED

Praise the LORD from the earth,
you great sea creatures and all ocean depths,
lightning and hail, snow and clouds,
stormy winds that do his bidding,
you mountains and all hills,
fruit trees and all cedars,
wild animals and all cattle,
small creatures and flying birds,
kings of the earth and all nations,
you princes and all rulers on earth,
young men and maidens,
old men and children.
Let them praise the name of the LORD,
for his name alone is exalted;
his splendor is above the earth and the heavens.

—PSALM 148:7-13

SWEET TO THE TASTE

Eat honey, my son, for it is good;
honey from the comb is sweet to your taste.
Know also that wisdom is sweet to your soul;
if you find it, there is a future hope for you,
and your hope will not be cut off.

—PROVERBS 24:13–14

I LOVE THOSE WHO LOVE ME

"I, wisdom, dwell together with prudence;
I possess knowledge and discretion.
To fear the LORD is to hate evil;
I hate pride and arrogance,
evil behavior and perverse speech.
Counsel and sound judgment are mine;
I have understanding and power.
By me kings reign
and rulers make laws that are just;
by me princes govern,
and all nobles who rule on earth.
I love those who love me,
and those who seek me find me.
With me are riches and honor,
enduring wealth and prosperity.
My fruit is better than fine gold;
what I yield surpasses choice silver.
I walk in the way of righteousness,
along the paths of justice,
bestowing wealth on those who love me
and making their treasuries full.

—PROVERBS 8:12-21

I WILL REBUKE YOU

But to the wicked, God says:
"What right have you to recite my laws
or take my covenant on your lips?
You hate my instruction
and cast my words behind you.
When you see a thief, you join with him;
you throw in your lot with adulterers.
You use your mouth for evil
and harness your tongue to deceit.
You speak continually against your brother
and slander your own mother's son.
These things you have done and I kept silent;
you thought I was altogether like you.
But I will rebuke you
and accuse you to your face.

—PSALM 50:16–21

❧ THE PEOPLES PLOT IN VAIN

Why do the nations conspire
and the peoples plot in vain?
The kings of the earth take their stand
and the rulers gather together
against the LORD and against his Anointed One.
"Let us break their chains," they say,
"and throw off their fetters."
The One enthroned in heaven laughs;
the Lord scoffs at them.

—PSALM 2:1-4

January 24

❧ Seven Things

There are six things the LORD hates,
seven that are detestable to him:
haughty eyes, a lying tongue,
hands that shed innocent blood,
a heart that devises wicked schemes,
feet that are quick to rush into evil,
a false witness who pours out lies
and a man who stirs up dissension among brothers.

—PROVERBS 6:16–19

✵ SHE KNOWS IT NOT

My son, pay attention to my wisdom,
listen well to my words of insight,
that you may maintain discretion
and your lips may preserve knowledge.
For the lips of an adulteress drip honey,
and her speech is smoother than oil;
but in the end she is bitter as gall,
sharp as a double-edged sword.
Her feet go down to death;
her steps lead straight to the grave.
She gives no thought to the way of life;
her paths are crooked, but she knows it not.

—PROVERBS 5:1-6

LIKE NEW GRASS

You turn men back to dust,
saying, "Return to dust, O sons of men."
For a thousand years in your sight
are like a day that has just gone by,
or like a watch in the night.
You sweep men away in the sleep of death;
they are like the new grass of the morning—
though in the morning it springs up new,
by evening it is dry and withered.

—PSALM 90:3–6

THE FIRST GLEAM OF DAWN

The path of the righteous
is like the first gleam of dawn,
shining ever brighter
till the full light of day.
But the way of the wicked
is like deep darkness;
they do not know
what makes them stumble.

—PROVERBS 4:18-19

FREEDOM

Be sure of this: The wicked will not go unpunished,
but those who are righteous will go free.
Like a gold ring in a pig's snout
is a beautiful woman who shows no discretion.
The desire of the righteous ends only in good,
but the hope of the wicked only in wrath.
One man gives freely, yet gains even more;
another withholds unduly, but comes to poverty.
A generous man will prosper;
he who refreshes others will himself be refreshed.
People curse the man who hoards grain,
but blessing crowns him who is willing to sell.
He who seeks good finds goodwill,
but evil comes to him who searches for it.

—PROVERBS 11:21–27

❧ TEACH ME

Show me your ways, O LORD,
teach me your paths;
guide me in your truth and teach me,
for you are God my Savior,
and my hope is in you all day long.
Remember, O LORD, your great mercy and love,
for they are from of old.
Remember not the sins of my youth
and my rebellious ways;
according to your love remember me,
for you are good, O LORD.

—PSALM 25:4-7

THE PERVERSENESS OF EVIL

Wisdom will save you from the ways of wicked men,
from men whose words are perverse,
who leave the straight paths to walk in dark ways,
who delight in doing wrong
and rejoice in the perverseness of evil,
whose paths are crooked
and who are devious in their ways.
It will save you also from the adulteress,
from the wayward wife with her seductive words,
who has left the partner of her youth
and ignored the covenant she made before God.
For her house leads down to death
and her paths to the spirits of the dead.
None who go to her return or attain the paths of life.
Thus you will walk in the ways of good men
and keep to the paths of the righteous.
For the upright will live in the land,
and the blameless will remain in it;
but the wicked will be cut off from the land,
and the unfaithful will be torn from it.

—PROVERBS 2:12–22

❧ PRUDENCE

The proverbs of Solomon son of David, king of Israel:
for attaining wisdom and discipline;
for understanding words of insight;
for acquiring a disciplined and prudent life,
doing what is right and just and fair;
for giving prudence to the simple,
knowledge and discretion to the young—
let the wise listen and add to their learning,
and let the discerning get guidance—
for understanding proverbs and parables,
the sayings and riddles of the wise.

—PROVERBS 1:1-6

WHO IS A TEACHER LIKE HIM?

"God is exalted in his power.
Who is a teacher like him?
Who has prescribed his ways for him,
or said to him, 'You have done wrong'?
Remember to extol his work,
which men have praised in song.
All mankind has seen it;
men gaze on it from afar.
How great is God—beyond our understanding!
The number of his years is past finding out.

—JOB 36:22-26

OPEN MY EYES

How can a young man keep his way pure?
By living according to your word.
I seek you with all my heart;
do not let me stray from your commands.
I have hidden your word in my heart
that I might not sin against you.
Praise be to you, O LORD;
teach me your decrees.
With my lips I recount
all the laws that come from your mouth.
I rejoice in following your statutes
as one rejoices in great riches.
I meditate on your precepts
and consider your ways.
I delight in your decrees;
I will not neglect your word.
Do good to your servant, and I will live;
I will obey your word.
Open my eyes that I may see
wonderful things in your law.
I am a stranger on earth;
do not hide your commands from me.

—PSALM 119:9–19

❧ THE LORD WILL HEAR

How long, O men, will you turn my glory into shame?
How long will you love delusions and seek false gods?
Know that the LORD has set apart the godly for himself;
the LORD will hear when I call to him.

—PSALM 4:2-3

HE JUDGES EVEN THE HIGHEST

"Can anyone teach knowledge to God,
since he judges even the highest?
One man dies in full vigor,
completely secure and at ease,
his body well nourished,
his bones rich with marrow.
Another man dies in bitterness of soul,
never having enjoyed anything good.
Side by side they lie in the dust,
and worms cover them both.

—JOB 21:22–26

THEIR PLANS COME TO NOTHING

Do not put your trust in princes,
in mortal men, who cannot save.
When their spirit departs, they return to the ground;
on that very day their plans come to nothing.

—PSALM 146:3-4

❧ WHAT IS MAN?

"What is man, that he could be pure,
or one born of woman, that he could be righteous?
If God places no trust in his holy ones,
if even the heavens are not pure in his eyes,
how much less man, who is vile and corrupt,
who drinks up evil like water!

—JOB 15:14–16

CREATE IN ME A PURE HEART

Create in me a pure heart, O God,
and renew a steadfast spirit within me.
Do not cast me from your presence
or take your Holy Spirit from me.
Restore to me the joy of your salvation
and grant me a willing spirit, to sustain me.
Then I will teach transgressors your ways,
and sinners will turn back to you.

—PSALM 51:10-13

HOW CAN WE SING?

By the rivers of Babylon we sat and wept
when we remembered Zion.
There on the poplars
we hung our harps,
for there our captors asked us for songs,
our tormentors demanded songs of joy;
they said, "Sing us one of the songs of Zion!"
How can we sing the songs of the LORD
while in a foreign land?
If I forget you, O Jerusalem,
may my right hand forget its skill.

—PSALM 137:1–5

❧ INTEGRITY

His wife said to him,
"Are you still holding on to your integrity?
Curse God and die!"
He replied,
"You are talking like a foolish woman.
Shall we accept good from God,
and not trouble?"

—JOB 2:9-10

LIKE A DESERT OWL

Hear my prayer, O LORD;
let my cry for help come to you.
Do not hide your face from me
when I am in distress.
Turn your ear to me;
when I call, answer me quickly.
For my days vanish like smoke;
my bones burn like glowing embers.
My heart is blighted and withered like grass;
I forget to eat my food.
Because of my loud groaning
I am reduced to skin and bones.
I am like a desert owl,
like an owl among the ruins.
I lie awake; I have become
like a bird alone on a roof.

—PSALM 102:1–7

❧ THE MAKER OF ALL THINGS

As you do not know the path of the wind,
or how the body is formed in a mother's womb,
so you cannot understand the work of God,
the Maker of all things.

—ECCLESIASTES 11:5

❧ RIGHTEOUSNESS AND JUSTICE

You rule over the surging sea;
when its waves mount up, you still them.
You crushed Rahab like one of the slain;
with your strong arm you scattered your enemies.
The heavens are yours, and yours also the earth;
you founded the world and all that is in it.
You created the north and the south;
Tabor and Hermon sing for joy at your name.
Your arm is endued with power;
your hand is strong, your right hand exalted.
Righteousness and justice
are the foundation of your throne;
love and faithfulness go before you.
Blessed are those who have learned to acclaim you,
who walk in the light of your presence, O LORD.
They rejoice in your name all day long;
they exult in your righteousness.
For you are their glory and strength,
and by your favor you exalt our horn.
Indeed, our shield belongs to the LORD,
our king to the Holy One of Israel.

—PSALM 89:9–18

❧ A GIFT OF GOD

Then I realized that it is good and proper
for a man to eat and drink,
and to find satisfaction
in his toilsome labor under the sun
during the few days of life God has given him—
for this is his lot.
Moreover, when God gives any man
wealth and possessions,
and enables him to enjoy them,
to accept his lot and be happy in his work—
this is a gift of God.
He seldom reflects on the days of his life,
because God keeps him occupied with gladness of heart.

—ECCLESIASTES 5:18-20

CLOTHED WITH JOY

To you, O LORD, I called;
to the Lord I cried for mercy:
"What gain is there in my destruction,
in my going down into the pit?
Will the dust praise you?
Will it proclaim your faithfulness?
Hear, O LORD, and be merciful to me;
O LORD, be my help."
You turned my wailing into dancing;
you removed my sackcloth and clothed me with joy,
that my heart may sing to you and not be silent.
O LORD my God, I will give you thanks forever.

—PSALM 30:8–12

TWO THINGS I ASK

"Two things I ask of you, O LORD;
do not refuse me before I die:
Keep falsehood and lies far from me;
give me neither poverty nor riches,
but give me only my daily bread.
Otherwise, I may have too much and disown you
and say, 'Who is the LORD?'
Or I may become poor and steal,
and so dishonor the name of my God.

—PROVERBS 30:7-9

WHERE IS YOUR GOD?

By day the LORD directs his love,
at night his song is with me—
a prayer to the God of my life.
I say to God my Rock,
"Why have you forgotten me?
Why must I go about mourning,
oppressed by the enemy?"
My bones suffer mortal agony
as my foes taunt me,
saying to me all day long,
"Where is your God?"
Why are you downcast, O my soul?
Why so disturbed within me?
Put your hope in God,
for I will yet praise him,
my Savior and my God.

—PSALM 42:8–11

❧ VICTORY RESTS WITH THE LORD

There is no wisdom, no insight, no plan
that can succeed against the LORD.
The horse is made ready for the day of battle,
but victory rests with the LORD.

—PROVERBS 21:30-31

A Vine out of Egypt

O Lord God Almighty,
how long will your anger smolder
against the prayers of your people?
You have fed them with the bread of tears;
you have made them drink tears by the bowlful.
You have made us a source of contention
to our neighbors,
and our enemies mock us.
Restore us, O God Almighty;
make your face shine upon us,
that we may be saved.
You brought a vine out of Egypt;
you drove out the nations and planted it.

—Psalm 80:4–8

YOU WILL RESTORE MY LIFE

Your righteousness reaches to the skies, O God,
you who have done great things.
Who, O God, is like you?
Though you have made me see troubles,
many and bitter,
you will restore my life again;
from the depths of the earth
you will again bring me up.
You will increase my honor
and comfort me once again.

—PSALM 71:19-21

FEBRUARY 20

 # SHAME AND DISGRACE

He who robs his father and drives out his mother
is a son who brings shame and disgrace.
Stop listening to instruction, my son,
and you will stray from the words of knowledge.

—PROVERBS 19:26–27

HE RISES AGAIN

Do not lie in wait like an outlaw
against a righteous man's house,
do not raid his dwelling place;
for though a righteous man falls seven times,
he rises again,
but the wicked are brought down by calamity.
Do not gloat when your enemy falls;
when he stumbles,
do not let your heart rejoice,
or the LORD will see and disapprove
and turn his wrath away from him.
Do not fret because of evil men
or be envious of the wicked,
for the evil man has no future hope,
and the lamp of the wicked will be snuffed out.

—PROVERBS 24:15-20

WHAT HAS BEEN WILL BE AGAIN

What does man gain from all his labor
at which he toils under the sun?
Generations come and generations go,
but the earth remains forever.
The sun rises and the sun sets,
and hurries back to where it rises.
The wind blows to the south and turns to the north;
round and round it goes, ever returning on its course.
All streams flow into the sea, yet the sea is never full.
To the place the streams come from,
there they return again.
All things are wearisome, more than one can say.
The eye never has enough of seeing,
nor the ear its fill of hearing.
What has been will be again,
what has been done will be done again;
there is nothing new under the sun.
Is there anything of which one can say,
"Look! This is something new"?
It was here already, long ago;
it was here before our time.
There is no remembrance of men of old,
and even those who are yet to come
will not be remembered by those who follow.

—ECCLESIASTES 1:3–11

❧ A HEART OF WISDOM

Who knows the power of your anger?
For your wrath is as great as the fear that is due you.
Teach us to number our days aright,
that we may gain a heart of wisdom.

—PSALM 90:11-12

THAT FOOD IS DECEPTIVE

When you sit to dine with a ruler,
note well what is before you,
and put a knife to your throat
if you are given to gluttony.
Do not crave his delicacies,
for that food is deceptive.

—PROVERBS 23:1–3

SEDUCTION

With persuasive words she led him astray;
she seduced him with her smooth talk.
All at once he followed her
like an ox going to the slaughter,
like a deer stepping into a noose
till an arrow pierces his liver,
like a bird darting into a snare,
little knowing it will cost him his life.

—PROVERBS 7:21-23

GIVE EAR TO MY PRAYER

Hear, O LORD, my righteous plea;
listen to my cry.
Give ear to my prayer—
it does not rise from deceitful lips.
May my vindication come from you;
may your eyes see what is right.
Though you probe my heart and examine me at night,
though you test me, you will find nothing;
I have resolved that my mouth will not sin.

—PSALM 17:1–3

❧ A Tree of Life

The fruit of the righteous is a tree of life,
and he who wins souls is wise.
If the righteous receive their due on earth,
how much more the ungodly and the sinner!

—Proverbs 11:30-31

NO HARM WILL BEFALL YOU

If you make the Most High your dwelling —
even the LORD, who is my refuge —
then no harm will befall you,
no disaster will come near your tent.
For he will command his angels concerning you
to guard you in all your ways;
they will lift you up in their hands,
so that you will not strike your foot against a stone.
You will tread upon the lion and the cobra;
you will trample the great lion and the serpent.

—PSALM 91:9–13

❧ MY ROCK

To you I call, O LORD my Rock;
do not turn a deaf ear to me.
For if you remain silent,
I will be like those who have gone down to the pit.
Hear my cry for mercy
as I call to you for help,
as I lift up my hands
toward your Most Holy Place.

—PSALM 28:1-2

❧ THE IDOLS OF THE NATIONS

Your name, O LORD, endures forever,
your renown, O LORD, through all generations.
For the LORD will vindicate his people
and have compassion on his servants.
The idols of the nations are silver and gold,
made by the hands of men.
They have mouths, but cannot speak,
eyes, but they cannot see;
they have ears, but cannot hear,
nor is there breath in their mouths.
Those who make them will be like them,
and so will all who trust in them.

—PSALM 135:13–18

ENJOY SAFE PASTURE

Do not fret because of evil men
or be envious of those who do wrong;
for like the grass they will soon wither,
like green plants they will soon die away.
Trust in the LORD *and do good;*
dwell in the land and enjoy safe pasture.
Delight yourself in the LORD
and he will give you the desires of your heart.

—PSALM 37:1–4

❧ MY GUILT IS NOT HIDDEN FROM YOU

Save me, O God,
for the waters have come up to my neck.
I sink in the miry depths,
where there is no foothold.
I have come into the deep waters;
the floods engulf me.
I am worn out calling for help;
my throat is parched.
My eyes fail,
looking for my God.
Those who hate me without reason
outnumber the hairs of my head;
many are my enemies without cause,
those who seek to destroy me.
I am forced to restore
what I did not steal.
You know my folly, O God;
my guilt is not hidden from you.

—PSALM 69:1–5

LET US EXAMINE OUR WAYS

Let us examine our ways and test them,
and let us return to the LORD.
Let us lift up our hearts and our hands
to God in heaven, and say:
"We have sinned and rebelled
and you have not forgiven.
"You have covered yourself with anger and pursued us;
you have slain without pity.
You have covered yourself with a cloud
so that no prayer can get through.
You have made us scum and refuse
among the nations.

—LAMENTATIONS 3:40–45

YOUR YEARS WILL NEVER END

In the course of my life he broke my strength;
he cut short my days.
So I said:
"Do not take me away, O my God,
in the midst of my days;
your years go on through all generations.
In the beginning you laid the foundations of the earth,
and the heavens are the work of your hands.
They will perish, but you remain;
they will all wear out like a garment.
Like clothing you will change them
and they will be discarded.
But you remain the same,
and your years will never end.
The children of your servants will live in your presence;
their descendants will be established before you."

—PSALM 102:23–28

I WILL CONFESS

Blessed is he
whose transgressions are forgiven,
whose sins are covered.
Blessed is the man
whose sin the LORD does not count against him
and in whose spirit is no deceit.
When I kept silent,
my bones wasted away
through my groaning all day long.
For day and night
your hand was heavy upon me;
my strength was sapped
as in the heat of summer.
Then I acknowledged my sin to you
and did not cover up my iniquity.
I said, "I will confess
my transgressions to the LORD"—
and you forgave
the guilt of my sin.

—PSALM 32:1–5

❧ HE FILLS HIS HANDS WITH LIGHTNING

"He draws up the drops of water,
which distill as rain to the streams;
the clouds pour down their moisture
and abundant showers fall on mankind.
Who can understand how he spreads out the clouds,
how he thunders from his pavilion?
See how he scatters his lightning about him,
bathing the depths of the sea.
This is the way he governs the nations
and provides food in abundance.
He fills his hands with lightning
and commands it to strike its mark.
His thunder announces the coming storm;
even the cattle make known its approach.

—JOB 36:27–33

HE RESCUED ME

He reached down from on high and took hold of me;
he drew me out of deep waters.
He rescued me from my powerful enemy,
from my foes, who were too strong for me.
They confronted me in the day of my disaster,
but the LORD was my support.
He brought me out into a spacious place;
he rescued me because he delighted in me.

—PSALM 18:16–19

❧ I CALLED TO YOU

I will exalt you, O LORD,
for you lifted me out of the depths
and did not let my enemies gloat over me.
O LORD my God, I called to you for help
and you healed me.
O LORD, you brought me up from the grave;
you spared me from going down into the pit.

—PSALM 30:1–3

MY LOVING GOD

They return at evening,
snarling like dogs,
and prowl about the city.
They wander about for food
and howl if not satisfied.
But I will sing of your strength,
in the morning I will sing of your love;
for you are my fortress,
my refuge in times of trouble.
O my Strength, I sing praise to you;
you, O God, are my fortress, my loving God.

—PSALM 59:14–17

❧ NO EYE WILL SEE ME

"There are those who rebel against the light,
who do not know its ways
or stay in its paths.
When daylight is gone, the murderer rises up
and kills the poor and needy;
in the night he steals forth like a thief.
The eye of the adulterer watches for dusk;
he thinks, 'No eye will see me,'
and he keeps his face concealed.
In the dark, men break into houses,
but by day they shut themselves in;
they want nothing to do with the light.
For all of them, deep darkness is their morning;
they make friends with the terrors of darkness.

—JOB 24:13–17

❧ LIKE OLIVE SHOOTS

Blessed are all who fear the LORD,
who walk in his ways.
You will eat the fruit of your labor;
blessings and prosperity will be yours.
Your wife will be like a fruitful vine within your house;
your sons will be like olive shoots around your table.
Thus is the man blessed
who fears the LORD.

—PSALM 128:1–4

❧ A MERE PHANTOM

"Show me, O LORD, my life's end
and the number of my days;
let me know how fleeting is my life.
You have made my days a mere handbreadth;
the span of my years is as nothing before you.
Each man's life is but a breath.
Man is a mere phantom as he goes to and fro:
He bustles about, but only in vain;
he heaps up wealth, not knowing who will get it.

—PSALM 39:4–6

THOSE WHO CURSE THEIR FATHERS

"There are those who curse their fathers
and do not bless their mothers;
those who are pure in their own eyes
and yet are not cleansed of their filth;
those whose eyes are ever so haughty,
whose glances are so disdainful;
those whose teeth are swords
and whose jaws are set with knives
to devour the poor from the earth,
the needy from among mankind.

—PROVERBS 30:11–14

❦ A CHASING AFTER THE WIND

I denied myself nothing my eyes desired;
I refused my heart no pleasure.
My heart took delight in all my work,
and this was the reward for all my labor.
Yet when I surveyed all that my hands had done
and what I had toiled to achieve,
everything was meaningless, a chasing after the wind;
nothing was gained under the sun.

—ECCLESIASTES 2:10–11

THE LORD WILL SUSTAIN AND RESTORE

Blessed is he who has regard for the weak;
the LORD delivers him in times of trouble.
The LORD will protect him and preserve his life;
he will bless him in the land
and not surrender him to the desire of his foes.
The LORD will sustain him on his sickbed
and restore him from his bed of illness.

—PSALM 41:1–3

HE FLATTERS HIMSELF

An oracle is within my heart
concerning the sinfulness of the wicked:
There is no fear of God before his eyes.
For in his own eyes he flatters himself
too much to detect or hate his sin.

—PSALM 36:1–2

❧ WHAT I DREADED HAS HAPPENED TO ME

Why is life given to a man
whose way is hidden,
whom God has hedged in?
For sighing comes to me instead of food;
my groans pour out like water.
What I feared has come upon me;
what I dreaded has happened to me.

—JOB 3:23–25

❧ SOW IN THE MORNING

Sow your seed in the morning,
and at evening let not your hands be idle,
for you do not know which will succeed,
whether this or that,
or whether both will do equally well.

—ECCLESIASTES 11:6

THE FOOD OF A STINGY MAN

Do not eat the food of a stingy man,
do not crave his delicacies;
for he is the kind of man
who is always thinking about the cost.
"Eat and drink," he says to you,
but his heart is not with you.
You will vomit up the little you have eaten
and will have wasted your compliments.

—PROVERBS 23:6–8

❧ THE WATERS FLOW

He sends his command to the earth;
his word runs swiftly.
He spreads the snow like wool
and scatters the frost like ashes.
He hurls down his hail like pebbles.
Who can withstand his icy blast?
He sends his word and melts them;
he stirs up his breezes, and the waters flow.

—PSALM 147:15–18

THE OIL OF JOY

Your throne, O God, will last for ever and ever;
a scepter of justice will be the scepter of your kingdom.
You love righteousness and hate wickedness;
therefore God, your God,
has set you above your companions
by anointing you with the oil of joy.

—PSALM 45:6–7

❧ GUIDE ME

You are God my stronghold.
Why have you rejected me?
Why must I go about mourning,
oppressed by the enemy?
Send forth your light and your truth,
let them guide me;
let them bring me to your holy mountain,
to the place where you dwell.
Then will I go to the altar of God,
to God, my joy and my delight.
I will praise you with the harp,
O God, my God.
Why are you downcast, O my soul?
Why so disturbed within me?
Put your hope in God,
for I will yet praise him,
my Savior and my God.

—PSALM 43:2–5

❧ LOVE AND FAITHFULNESS

My son, do not forget my teaching,
but keep my commands in your heart,
for they will prolong your life many years
and bring you prosperity.
Let love and faithfulness never leave you;
bind them around your neck,
write them on the tablet of your heart.
Then you will win favor and a good name
in the sight of God and man.

—PROVERBS 3:1–4

STOP AND CONSIDER GOD'S WONDERS

"Listen to this, Job;
stop and consider God's wonders.

"Tell us what we should say to him;
we cannot draw up our case because of our darkness.
Should he be told that I want to speak?
Would any man ask to be swallowed up?
Now no one can look at the sun,
bright as it is in the skies
after the wind has swept them clean.
Out of the north he comes in golden splendor;
God comes in awesome majesty.
The Almighty is beyond our reach
and exalted in power;
in his justice and great righteousness,
he does not oppress.
Therefore, men revere him,
for does he not have regard for all the wise in heart?"

—JOB 37:14, 19–24

❧ SCORNED AND DESPISED

But I am a worm and not a man,
scorned by men and despised by the people.
All who see me mock me;
they hurl insults, shaking their heads:
"He trusts in the LORD;
let the LORD rescue him.
Let him deliver him,
since he delights in him."

—PSALM 22:6–8

❧ THE LENGTH OF OUR DAYS

We are consumed by your anger
and terrified by your indignation.
You have set our iniquities before you,
our secret sins in the light of your presence.
All our days pass away under your wrath;
we finish our years with a moan.
The length of our days is seventy years—
or eighty, if we have the strength;
yet their span is but trouble and sorrow,
for they quickly pass, and we fly away.

—PSALM 90:7–10

❦ DOES NOT WISDOM CALL OUT?

Does not wisdom call out?
Does not understanding raise her voice?
On the heights along the way, where the paths meet,
she takes her stand;
beside the gates leading into the city, at the entrances,
she cries aloud: "To you, O men, I call out;
I raise my voice to all mankind.
You who are simple, gain prudence;
you who are foolish, gain understanding.
Listen, for I have worthy things to say;
I open my lips to speak what is right.
My mouth speaks what is true,
for my lips detest wickedness.
All the words of my mouth are just;
none of them is crooked or perverse.
To the discerning all of them are right;
they are faultless to those who have knowledge.
Choose my instruction instead of silver,
knowledge rather than choice gold,
for wisdom is more precious than rubies,
and nothing you desire can compare with her.
"I, wisdom, dwell together with prudence;
I possess knowledge and discretion.
To fear the LORD is to hate evil;
I hate pride and arrogance,
evil behavior and perverse speech.

—PROVERBS 8:1–13

❧ MAKE THE RIGHTEOUS SECURE

Let the assembled peoples gather around you.
Rule over them from on high;
let the LORD judge the peoples.
Judge me, O LORD, according to my righteousness,
according to my integrity, O Most High.
O righteous God,
who searches minds and hearts,
bring to an end the violence of the wicked
and make the righteous secure.

—PSALM 7:7–9

BY WHAT HE HAS DONE

If you say, "But we knew nothing about this,"
does not he who weighs the heart perceive it?
Does not he who guards your life know it?
Will he not repay each person
according to what he has done?

—PROVERBS 24:12

❧ MY SONGS IN THE NIGHT

I cried out to God for help;
I cried out to God to hear me.
When I was in distress, I sought the Lord;
at night I stretched out untiring hands
and my soul refused to be comforted.
I remembered you, O God, and I groaned;
I mused, and my spirit grew faint.
You kept my eyes from closing;
I was too troubled to speak.
I thought about the former days,
the years of long ago;
I remembered my songs in the night.
My heart mused and my spirit inquired:
"Will the Lord reject forever?
Will he never show his favor again?
Has his unfailing love vanished forever?
Has his promise failed for all time?
Has God forgotten to be merciful?
Has he in anger withheld his compassion?"

—PSALM 77:1–9

THE WINTER IS PAST

My lover spoke and said to me,
"Arise, my darling,
my beautiful one, and come with me.
See! The winter is past;
the rains are over and gone.
Flowers appear on the earth;
the season of singing has come,
the cooing of doves
is heard in our land.
The fig tree forms its early fruit;
the blossoming vines spread their fragrance.
Arise, come, my darling;
my beautiful one, come with me."

—SONG OF SONGS 2:10–13

THEY CRIED OUT TO THE LORD

Others went out on the sea in ships;
they were merchants on the mighty waters.
They saw the works of the LORD,
his wonderful deeds in the deep.
For he spoke and stirred up a tempest
that lifted high the waves.
They mounted up to the heavens and
went down to the depths;
in their peril their courage melted away.
They reeled and staggered like drunken men;
they were at their wits' end.
Then they cried out to the LORD in their trouble,
and he brought them out of their distress.
He stilled the storm to a whisper;
the waves of the sea were hushed.
They were glad when it grew calm,
and he guided them to their desired haven.
Let them give thanks to the LORD for his unfailing love
and his wonderful deeds for men.

—PSALM 107:23–31

❧ WHERE WERE YOU?

Then the LORD answered Job out of the storm.
He said: "Who is this that darkens my counsel
with words without knowledge?
Brace yourself like a man;
I will question you,
and you shall answer me.
"Where were you when I laid the earth's foundation?
Tell me, if you understand.
Who marked off its dimensions? Surely you know!
Who stretched a measuring line across it?
On what were its footings set,
or who laid its cornerstone—
while the morning stars sang together
and all the angels shouted for joy?
—JOB 38:1–7

I Am in Trouble

But I pray to you, O LORD,
in the time of your favor;
in your great love, O God,
answer me with your sure salvation.
Rescue me from the mire,
do not let me sink;
deliver me from those who hate me,
from the deep waters.
Do not let the floodwaters engulf me
or the depths swallow me up
or the pit close its mouth over me.
Answer me, O LORD, out of the goodness of your love;
in your great mercy turn to me.
Do not hide your face from your servant;
answer me quickly, for I am in trouble.
Come near and rescue me;
redeem me because of my foes.

—PSALM 69:13–18

❧ I WILL WALK IN YOUR TRUTH

Teach me your way, O LORD,
and I will walk in your truth;
give me an undivided heart,
that I may fear your name.
I will praise you, O Lord my God, with all my heart;
I will glorify your name forever.
For great is your love toward me;
you have delivered me from the depths of the grave.

—PSALM 86:11–13

As Surely As God Lives

"As surely as God lives, who has denied me justice,
the Almighty, who has made me taste bitterness of soul,
as long as I have life within me,
the breath of God in my nostrils,
my lips will not speak wickedness,
and my tongue will utter no deceit.
I will never admit you are in the right;
till I die, I will not deny my integrity.
I will maintain my righteousness and never let go of it;
my conscience will not reproach me as long as I live.

—Job 27:2–6

❧ LIKE THE NOONDAY SUN

Commit your way to the LORD;
trust in him and he will do this:
He will make your righteousness shine like the dawn,
the justice of your cause like the noonday sun.
Be still before the LORD and wait patiently for him;
do not fret when men succeed in their ways,
when they carry out their wicked schemes.

—PSALM 37:5–7

FREE YOURSELF

My son, if you have put up security for your neighbor,
if you have struck hands in pledge for another,
if you have been trapped by what you said,
ensnared by the words of your mouth,
then do this, my son, to free yourself,
since you have fallen into your neighbor's hands:
Go and humble yourself;
press your plea with your neighbor!
Allow no sleep to your eyes,
no slumber to your eyelids.
Free yourself,
like a gazelle from the hand of the hunter,
like a bird from the snare of the fowler.

—PROVERBS 6:1–5

❧ LET US REJOICE AND BE GLAD IN IT

The stone the builders rejected
has become the capstone;
the LORD has done this,
and it is marvelous in our eyes.
This is the day the LORD has made;
let us rejoice and be glad in it.

—PSALM 118:22–24

MY REDEEMER LIVES

"Oh, that my words were recorded,
that they were written on a scroll,
that they were inscribed with an iron tool on lead,
or engraved in rock forever!
I know that my Redeemer lives,
and that in the end he will stand upon the earth.
And after my skin has been destroyed,
yet in my flesh I will see God;
I myself will see him
with my own eyes—I, and not another.
How my heart yearns within me!

—JOB 19:23–27

❧ LET ME NOT EAT OF THEIR DELICACIES

Set a guard over my mouth, O LORD;
keep watch over the door of my lips.
Let not my heart be drawn to what is evil,
to take part in wicked deeds
with men who are evildoers;
let me not eat of their delicacies.

—PSALM 141:3–4

FOOLS DESPISE WISDOM

The fear of the LORD is the beginning of knowledge,
but fools despise wisdom and discipline.
Listen, my son, to your father's instruction
and do not forsake your mother's teaching.

—PROVERBS 1:7–8

❧ MIGHTY IN POWER

He determines the number of the stars
and calls them each by name.
Great is our Lord and mighty in power;
his understanding has no limit.

—PSALM 147:4–5

I HEARD A HUSHED VOICE

"A word was secretly brought to me,
my ears caught a whisper of it.
Amid disquieting dreams in the night,
when deep sleep falls on men,
fear and trembling seized me
and made all my bones shake.
A spirit glided past my face,
and the hair on my body stood on end.
It stopped, but I could not tell what it was.
A form stood before my eyes,
and I heard a hushed voice:
'Can a mortal be more righteous than God?
Can a man be more pure than his Maker?

—JOB 4:12–17

WISDOM IS A SHELTER

Wisdom, like an inheritance, is a good thing
and benefits those who see the sun.
Wisdom is a shelter as money is a shelter,
but the advantage of knowledge is this:
that wisdom preserves the life of its possessor.

—ECCLESIASTES 7:11–12

I CALLED TO THE LORD

I call to the LORD, who is worthy of praise,
and I am saved from my enemies.
The cords of death entangled me;
the torrents of destruction overwhelmed me.
The cords of the grave coiled around me;
the snares of death confronted me.
In my distress I called to the LORD;
I cried to my God for help.

—PSALM 18:3–6

✻ A CHASING AFTER THE WIND

A man can do nothing better than to eat and drink
and find satisfaction in his work.
This too, I see, is from the hand of God,
for without him, who can eat or find enjoyment?
To the man who pleases him,
God gives wisdom, knowledge and happiness,
but to the sinner he gives the task of gathering
and storing up wealth to hand it over
to the one who pleases God.
This too is meaningless, a chasing after the wind.

—ECCLESIASTES 2:24–26

PREGNANT WITH EVIL

He who is pregnant with evil
and conceives trouble gives birth to disillusionment.
He who digs a hole and scoops it out
falls into the pit he has made.
The trouble he causes recoils on himself;
his violence comes down on his own head.

—PSALM 7:14–16

Shout with Joy to God

Shout with joy to God, all the earth!
Sing the glory of his name;
make his praise glorious!
Say to God, "How awesome are your deeds!
So great is your power
that your enemies cringe before you.
All the earth bows down to you;
they sing praise to you,
they sing praise to your name."

—Psalm 66:1–4

A Little Sleep

I went past the field of the sluggard,
past the vineyard of the man who lacks judgment;
thorns had come up everywhere,
the ground was covered with weeds,
and the stone wall was in ruins.
I applied my heart to what I observed
and learned a lesson from what I saw:
A little sleep, a little slumber,
a little folding of the hands to rest—
and poverty will come on you like a bandit
and scarcity like an armed man.

—Proverbs 24:30–34

❧ He Guards the Lives

Let those who love the LORD hate evil,
for he guards the lives of his faithful ones
and delivers them from the hand of the wicked.
Light is shed upon the righteous
and joy on the upright in heart.
Rejoice in the LORD, you who are righteous,
and praise his holy name.

—PSALM 97:10–12

❧ RARE AND BEAUTIFUL TREASURES

By wisdom a house is built,
and through understanding it is established;
through knowledge its rooms are filled
with rare and beautiful treasures.

—PROVERBS 24:3–4

❃ AN ANCIENT BOUNDARY STONE

Do not move an ancient boundary stone
or encroach on the fields of the fatherless,
for their Defender is strong;
he will take up their case against you.

—PROVERBS 23:10–11

I HAVE SINNED

I said, "O LORD, have mercy on me;
heal me, for I have sinned against you."

—PSALM 41:4

THREE THINGS

"The leech has two daughters.
'Give! Give!' they cry.
"There are three things that are never satisfied,
four that never say, 'Enough!':
the grave, the barren womb,
land, which is never satisfied with water,
and fire, which never says, 'Enough!'

—PROVERBS 30:15–16

MY SOUL THIRSTS FOR YOU

O God, you are my God,
earnestly I seek you;
my soul thirsts for you,
my body longs for you,
in a dry and weary land
where there is no water.

—PSALM 63:1

❧ WHO CAN STAND BEFORE JEALOUSY?

Anger is cruel and fury overwhelming,
but who can stand before jealousy?

—PROVERBS 27:4

HIS HOLY MOUNTAIN

Great is the LORD, and most worthy of praise,
in the city of our God, his holy mountain.
It is beautiful in its loftiness,
the joy of the whole earth.
Like the utmost heights of Zaphon is Mount Zion,
the city of the Great King.
God is in her citadels;
he has shown himself to be her fortress.

—PSALM 48:1–3

❧ THOUGH HE SLAY ME

"Keep silent and let me speak;
then let come to me what may.
Why do I put myself in jeopardy
and take my life in my hands?
Though he slay me, yet will I hope in him;
I will surely defend my ways to his face.
Indeed, this will turn out for my deliverance,
for no godless man would dare come before him!
Listen carefully to my words;
let your ears take in what I say.
Now that I have prepared my case,
I know I will be vindicated.
Can anyone bring charges against me?
If so, I will be silent and die.

—JOB 13:13–19

WHY DO YOU REJECT ME?

Why, O LORD, do you reject me
and hide your face from me?
From my youth I have been afflicted and close to death;
I have suffered your terrors and am in despair.
Your wrath has swept over me;
your terrors have destroyed me.
All day long they surround me like a flood;
they have completely engulfed me.
You have taken my companions and loved ones from me;
the darkness is my closest friend.

—PSALM 88:14–18

❧ THAT IS WISDOM

"Where then does wisdom come from?
Where does understanding dwell?
It is hidden from the eyes of every living thing,
concealed even from the birds of the air.
Destruction and Death say,
'Only a rumor of it has reached our ears.'
God understands the way to it
and he alone knows where it dwells,
for he views the ends of the earth
and sees everything under the heavens.
When he established the force of the wind
and measured out the waters,
when he made a decree for the rain
and a path for the thunderstorm,
then he looked at wisdom and appraised it;
he confirmed it and tested it.
And he said to man,
'The fear of the Lord—that is wisdom,
and to shun evil is understanding.'"

—JOB 28:20–28

❧ YOU SHOW YOURSELF SHREWD

To the faithful you show yourself faithful,
to the blameless you show yourself blameless,
to the pure you show yourself pure,
but to the crooked you show yourself shrewd.

—PSALM 18:25–26

❧ HONORED AMONG MEN

O LORD, you will keep us safe
and protect us from such people forever.
The wicked freely strut about
when what is vile is honored among men.

—PSALM 12:7–8

THROUGH ALL GENERATIONS

Shout for joy to the LORD, all the earth.
Worship the LORD with gladness;
come before him with joyful songs.
Know that the LORD is God.
It is he who made us, and we are his;
we are his people, the sheep of his pasture.
Enter his gates with thanksgiving
and his courts with praise;
give thanks to him and praise his name.
For the LORD is good and his love endures forever;
his faithfulness continues through all generations.

—PSALM 100:1–5

THEIR SONGS GROW FAINT

Remember your Creator in the days of your youth,
before the days of trouble come
and the years approach when you will say,
"I find no pleasure in them"—
before the sun and the light and the moon
and the stars grow dark,
and the clouds return after the rain;
when the keepers of the house tremble,
and the strong men stoop,
when the grinders cease because they are few,
and those looking through the windows grow dim;
when the doors to the street are closed
and the sound of grinding fades;
when men rise up at the sound of birds,
but all their songs grow faint;
when men are afraid of heights
and of dangers in the streets;
when the almond tree blossoms
and the grasshopper drags himself along
and desire no longer is stirred.
Then man goes to his eternal home
and mourners go about the streets.

—ECCLESIASTES 12:1–5

IF I HAD CHERISHED SIN

Come and listen, all you who fear God;
let me tell you what he has done for me.
I cried out to him with my mouth;
his praise was on my tongue.
If I had cherished sin in my heart,
the Lord would not have listened;
but God has surely listened
and heard my voice in prayer.
Praise be to God,
who has not rejected my prayer
or withheld his love from me!

—PSALM 66:16–20

❧ CAPTIVATED BY HER LOVE

Drink water from your own cistern,
running water from your own well.
Should your springs overflow in the streets,
your streams of water in the public squares?
Let them be yours alone,
never to be shared with strangers.
May your fountain be blessed,
and may you rejoice in the wife of your youth.
A loving doe, a graceful deer—
may her breasts satisfy you always,
may you ever be captivated by her love.
Why be captivated, my son, by an adulteress?
Why embrace the bosom of another man's wife?

—PROVERBS 5:15–20

❧ COME, MY LOVER

Come, my lover, let us go to the countryside,
let us spend the night in the villages.
Let us go early to the vineyards
to see if the vines have budded,
if their blossoms have opened,
and if the pomegranates are in bloom—
there I will give you my love.
The mandrakes send out their fragrance,
and at our door is every delicacy,
both new and old,
that I have stored up for you, my lover.

—SONG OF SONGS 7:11–13

We Will Tell the Next Generation

O my people, hear my teaching;
listen to the words of my mouth.
I will open my mouth in parables,
I will utter hidden things, things from of old—
what we have heard and known,
what our fathers have told us.
We will not hide them from their children;
we will tell the next generation
the praiseworthy deeds of the LORD,
his power, and the wonders he has done.

—PSALM 78:1–4

THE VAST EXPANSES OF THE EARTH

"Have you journeyed to the springs of the sea
or walked in the recesses of the deep?
Have the gates of death been shown to you?
Have you seen the gates of the shadow of death?
Have you comprehended the vast expanses of the earth?
Tell me, if you know all this.

—JOB 38:16–18

A Season for Every Activity under Heaven

There is a time for everything,
and a season for every activity under heaven:
a time to be born and a time to die,
a time to plant and a time to uproot,
a time to kill and a time to heal,
a time to tear down and a time to build,
a time to weep and a time to laugh,
a time to mourn and a time to dance,
a time to scatter stones and a time to gather them,
a time to embrace and a time to refrain,
a time to search and a time to give up,
a time to keep and a time to throw away,
a time to tear and a time to mend,
a time to be silent and a time to speak,
a time to love and a time to hate,
a time for war and a time for peace.

—Ecclesiastes 3:1–8

DO NOT RESENT HIS REBUKE

My son, do not despise the LORD's discipline
and do not resent his rebuke,
because the LORD disciplines those he loves,
as a father the son he delights in.

—PROVERBS 3:11–12

❧ LIKE A WEANED CHILD

My heart is not proud, O LORD,
my eyes are not haughty;
I do not concern myself with great matters
or things too wonderful for me.
But I have stilled and quieted my soul;
like a weaned child with its mother,
like a weaned child is my soul within me.
O Israel, put your hope in the LORD
both now and forevermore.

—PSALM 131:1–3

❧ CONSIDER WHAT GOD HAS DONE

Consider what God has done:
Who can straighten
what he has made crooked?
When times are good, be happy;
but when times are bad, consider:
God has made the one
as well as the other.
Therefore, a man cannot discover
anything about his future.

—ECCLESIASTES 7:13–14

❧ MY VIGOROUS ENEMIES

For I am about to fall,
and my pain is ever with me.
I confess my iniquity;
I am troubled by my sin.
Many are those who are my vigorous enemies;
those who hate me without reason are numerous.
Those who repay my good with evil
slander me when I pursue what is good.

—PSALM 38:17–20

FOUR THINGS

"There are three things that are too amazing for me,
four that I do not understand:
the way of an eagle in the sky,
the way of a snake on a rock,
the way of a ship on the high seas,
and the way of a man with a maiden.

—PROVERBS 30:18–19

✣ SAVE HIS SOUL

Do not withhold discipline from a child;
if you punish him with the rod, he will not die.
Punish him with the rod
and save his soul from death.

—PROVERBS 23:13–14

BE THEIR SHEPHERD

Praise be to the LORD,
for he has heard my cry for mercy.
The LORD is my strength and my shield;
my heart trusts in him, and I am helped.
My heart leaps for joy
and I will give thanks to him in song.
The LORD is the strength of his people,
a fortress of salvation for his anointed one.
Save your people and bless your inheritance;
be their shepherd and carry them forever.

—PSALM 28:6–9

❧ GUARD MY LIFE

Turn to me and be gracious to me,
for I am lonely and afflicted.
The troubles of my heart have multiplied;
free me from my anguish.
Look upon my affliction and my distress
and take away all my sins.
See how my enemies have increased
and how fiercely they hate me!
Guard my life and rescue me;
let me not be put to shame,
for I take refuge in you.
May integrity and uprightness protect me,
because my hope is in you.

—PSALM 25:16–21

❧ ONE MAN PRETENDS

One man pretends to be rich, yet has nothing;
another pretends to be poor, yet has great wealth.
A man's riches may ransom his life,
but a poor man hears no threat.

—PROVERBS 13:7–8

❧ As the Day Was Fading

At the window of my house
I looked out through the lattice.
I saw among the simple,
I noticed among the young men,
a youth who lacked judgment.
He was going down the street near her corner,
walking along in the direction of her house
at twilight, as the day was fading,
as the dark of night set in.

—Proverbs 7:6–9

❧ I Lift up My Eyes to You

I lift up my eyes to you,
to you whose throne is in heaven.
As the eyes of slaves look to the hand of their master,
as the eyes of a maid look to the hand of her mistress,
so our eyes look to the LORD our God,
till he shows us his mercy.
Have mercy on us, O LORD, have mercy on us,
for we have endured much contempt.
We have endured much ridicule from the proud,
much contempt from the arrogant.

—PSALM 123:1–4

❧ GUARD YOUR HEART

My son, pay attention to what I say;
listen closely to my words.
Do not let them out of your sight,
keep them within your heart;
for they are life to those who find them
and health to a man's whole body.
Above all else, guard your heart,
for it is the wellspring of life.
Put away perversity from your mouth;
keep corrupt talk far from your lips.
Let your eyes look straight ahead,
fix your gaze directly before you.
Make level paths for your feet
and take only ways that are firm.
Do not swerve to the right or the left;
keep your foot from evil.

—PROVERBS 4:20–27

HARD SERVICE

"Does not man have hard service on earth?
Are not his days like those of a hired man?
Like a slave longing for the evening shadows,
or a hired man waiting eagerly for his wages,
so I have been allotted months of futility,
and nights of misery have been assigned to me.
When I lie down I think, 'How long before I get up?'
The night drags on, and I toss till dawn.
My body is clothed with worms and scabs,
my skin is broken and festering.

—JOB 7:1–5

❧ In His Word I Put My Hope

Out of the depths I cry to you, O LORD;
O Lord, hear my voice.
Let your ears be attentive
to my cry for mercy.

If you, O LORD, kept a record of sins,
O Lord, who could stand?
But with you there is forgiveness;
therefore you are feared.
I wait for the LORD, my soul waits,
and in his word I put my hope.
My soul waits for the Lord
more than watchmen wait for the morning,
more than watchmen wait for the morning.

—PSALM 130:1–6

DECEIT IN HIS HEART

A scoundrel and villain,
who goes about with a corrupt mouth,
who winks with his eye,
signals with his feet
and motions with his fingers,
who plots evil with deceit in his heart—
he always stirs up dissension.
Therefore disaster will overtake him in an instant;
he will suddenly be destroyed—without remedy.

—PROVERBS 6:12–15

SPRINGS OF WATER

The sea looked and fled,
the Jordan turned back;
the mountains skipped like rams,
the hills like lambs.
Why was it, O sea, that you fled,
O Jordan, that you turned back,
you mountains, that you skipped like rams,
you hills, like lambs?
Tremble, O earth, at the presence of the Lord,
at the presence of the God of Jacob,
who turned the rock into a pool,
the hard rock into springs of water.

—PSALM 114:3–8

A WAY THAT SEEMS RIGHT

The highway of the upright avoids evil;
he who guards his way guards his life.
Pride goes before destruction,
a haughty spirit before a fall.
There is a way that seems right to a man,
but in the end it leads to death.

—PROVERBS 16:17, 18, 25

THE KNOWLEDGE OF GOD

My son, if you accept my words
and store up my commands within you,
turning your ear to wisdom
and applying your heart to understanding,
and if you call out for insight
and cry aloud for understanding,
and if you look for it as for silver
and search for it as for hidden treasure,
then you will understand the fear of the LORD
and find the knowledge of God.

—PROVERBS 2:1–5

IN YOUR NAME I WILL HOPE

The righteous will see and fear;
they will laugh at him, saying,
"Here now is the man
who did not make God his stronghold
but trusted in his great wealth
and grew strong by destroying others!"
But I am like an olive tree
flourishing in the house of God;
I trust in God's unfailing love
for ever and ever.
I will praise you forever for what you have done;
in your name I will hope, for your name is good.
I will praise you in the presence of your saints.

—PSALM 52:6–9

HE WHO PURSUES RIGHTEOUSNESS FINDS LIFE

When justice is done, it brings joy to the righteous
but terror to evildoers.
A man who strays from the path of understanding
comes to rest in the company of the dead.
He who loves pleasure will become poor;
whoever loves wine and oil will never be rich.
The wicked become a ransom for the righteous,
and the unfaithful for the upright.
Better to live in a desert
than with a quarrelsome and ill-tempered wife.
In the house of the wise are stores of choice food and oil,
but a foolish man devours all he has.
He who pursues righteousness and love
finds life, prosperity and honor.

—PROVERBS 21:15–21

❧ ETERNITY IN THE HEARTS OF MEN

What does the worker gain from his toil?
I have seen the burden God has laid on men.
He has made everything beautiful in its time.
He has also set eternity in the hearts of men;
yet they cannot fathom what God has done
from beginning to end.

—ECCLESIASTES 3:9–11

THE SEA IS HIS, FOR HE MADE IT

Come, let us sing for joy to the LORD;
let us shout aloud to the Rock of our salvation.
Let us come before him with thanksgiving
and extol him with music and song.
For the LORD is the great God,
the great King above all gods.
In his hand are the depths of the earth,
and the mountain peaks belong to him.
The sea is his, for he made it,
and his hands formed the dry land.
Come, let us bow down in worship,
let us kneel before the LORD our Maker;
for he is our God
and we are the people of his pasture,
the flock under his care.

—PSALM 95:1–7

THEY DID NOT BELIEVE

In spite of all this, they kept on sinning;
in spite of his wonders, they did not believe.
So he ended their days in futility
and their years in terror.
Whenever God slew them, they would seek him;
they eagerly turned to him again.
They remembered that God was their Rock,
that God Most High was their Redeemer.
But then they would flatter him with their mouths,
lying to him with their tongues;
their hearts were not loyal to him,
they were not faithful to his covenant.
Yet he was merciful;
he forgave their iniquities
and did not destroy them.
Time after time he restrained his anger
and did not stir up his full wrath.
He remembered that they were but flesh,
a passing breeze that does not return.
—PSALM 78:32–39

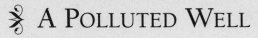

A POLLUTED WELL

Like a muddied spring or a polluted well
is a righteous man who gives way to the wicked.

—PROVERBS 25:26

I ENVIED THE ARROGANT

But as for me, my feet had almost slipped;
I had nearly lost my foothold.
For I envied the arrogant
when I saw the prosperity of the wicked.
They have no struggles;
their bodies are healthy and strong.
They are free from the burdens common to man;
they are not plagued by human ills.
Therefore pride is their necklace;
they clothe themselves with violence.
From their callous hearts comes iniquity;
the evil conceits of their minds know no limits.
They scoff, and speak with malice;
in their arrogance they threaten oppression.
Their mouths lay claim to heaven,
and their tongues take possession of the earth.
Therefore their people turn to them
and drink up waters in abundance.
They say, "How can God know?
Does the Most High have knowledge?"
This is what the wicked are like—
always carefree, they increase in wealth.
Surely in vain have I kept my heart pure;
in vain have I washed my hands in innocence.
All day long I have been plagued;
I have been punished every morning.

—PSALM 73:2–14

THE FOOL

Like snow in summer or rain in harvest,
honor is not fitting for a fool.
Like a fluttering sparrow or a darting swallow,
an undeserved curse does not come to rest.
A whip for the horse, a halter for the donkey,
and a rod for the backs of fools!
Do not answer a fool according to his folly,
or you will be like him yourself.

—PROVERBS 26:1–4

❧ IN HOLY MAJESTY

The LORD will extend your mighty scepter from Zion;
you will rule in the midst of your enemies.
Your troops will be willing
on your day of battle.
Arrayed in holy majesty,
from the womb of the dawn
you will receive the dew of your youth.

—PSALM 110:2–3

Who Endowed the Heart with Wisdom?

"Can you raise your voice to the clouds
and cover yourself with a flood of water?
Do you send the lightning bolts on their way?
Do they report to you, 'Here we are'?
Who endowed the heart with wisdom
or gave understanding to the mind?
Who has the wisdom to count the clouds?
Who can tip over the water jars of the heavens
when the dust becomes hard
and the clods of earth stick together?

—Job 38:34–38

YOUR WAYS MAY BE KNOWN

May God be gracious to us and bless us
and make his face shine upon us,
that your ways may be known on earth,
your salvation among all nations.

—PSALM 67:1–2

JUST THE RIGHT WORDS

Not only was the Teacher wise,
but also he imparted knowledge to the people.
He pondered and searched out
and set in order many proverbs.
The Teacher searched to find just the right words,
and what he wrote was upright and true.
The words of the wise are like goads,
their collected sayings like firmly embedded nails—
given by one Shepherd.
Be warned, my son, of anything in addition to them.
Of making many books there is no end,
and much study wearies the body.

—ECCLESIASTES 12:9–12

✳ RESCUE ME

Rescue me, O LORD, from evil men;
protect me from men of violence,
who devise evil plans in their hearts
and stir up war every day.
They make their tongues as sharp as a serpent's;
the poison of vipers is on their lips.
Keep me, O LORD, from the hands of the wicked;
protect me from men of violence
who plan to trip my feet.
Proud men have hidden a snare for me;
they have spread out the cords of their net
and have set traps for me along my path.

—PSALM 140:1–5

THE WICKED LIE IN WAIT

The wicked lie in wait for the righteous,
seeking their very lives;
but the LORD will not leave them in their power
or let them be condemned when brought to trial.

—PSALM 37:32–33

My Life Is but a Breath

"My days are swifter than a weaver's shuttle,
and they come to an end without hope.
Remember, O God, that my life is but a breath;
my eyes will never see happiness again.
The eye that now sees me will see me no longer;
you will look for me, but I will be no more.
As a cloud vanishes and is gone,
so he who goes down to the grave does not return.
He will never come to his house again;
his place will know him no more.

—JOB 7:6–10

❧ LOVE IS AS STRONG AS DEATH

Who is this coming up from the desert
leaning on her lover?
Under the apple tree I roused you;
there your mother conceived you,
there she who was in labor gave you birth.
Place me like a seal over your heart,
like a seal on your arm;
for love is as strong as death,
its jealousy unyielding as the grave.
It burns like blazing fire,
like a mighty flame.
Many waters cannot quench love;
rivers cannot wash it away.
If one were to give
all the wealth of his house for love,
it would be utterly scorned.

—SONG OF SONGS 8:5–7

❧ SING TO HIM, SING PRAISE TO HIM

Give thanks to the LORD, call on his name;
make known among the nations what he has done.
Sing to him, sing praise to him;
tell of all his wonderful acts.
Glory in his holy name;
let the hearts of those who seek the LORD rejoice.
Look to the LORD and his strength;
seek his face always.
Remember the wonders he has done,
his miracles, and the judgments he pronounced.

—PSALM 105:1–5

Too Much Wine

Listen, my son, and be wise,
and keep your heart on the right path.
Do not join those who drink too much wine
or gorge themselves on meat,
for drunkards and gluttons become poor,
and drowsiness clothes them in rags.

—PROVERBS 23:19–21

WITH YOU THE WICKED CANNOT DWELL

You are not a God who takes pleasure in evil;
with you the wicked cannot dwell.
The arrogant cannot stand in your presence;
you hate all who do wrong.
You destroy those who tell lies;
bloodthirsty and deceitful men
the LORD abhors.

—PSALM 5:4–6

IN MY PRIME

Job continued his discourse:
"How I long for the months gone by,
for the days when God watched over me,
when his lamp shone upon my head
and by his light I walked through darkness!
Oh, for the days when I was in my prime,
when God's intimate friendship blessed my house,
when the Almighty was still with me
and my children were around me,
when my path was drenched with cream
and the rock poured out for me streams of olive oil.

—JOB 29:1–6

THE RIVERS CLAP THEIR HANDS

Let the sea resound, and everything in it,
the world, and all who live in it.
Let the rivers clap their hands,
let the mountains sing together for joy;
let them sing before the LORD,
for he comes to judge the earth.
He will judge the world in righteousness
and the peoples with equity.

—PSALM 98:7–9

EVERY KIND OF INCENSE TREE

You are a garden locked up,
my sister, my bride;
you are a spring enclosed,
a sealed fountain.
Your plants are an orchard of pomegranates
with choice fruits,
with henna and nard,
nard and saffron,
calamus and cinnamon,
with every kind of incense tree,
with myrrh and aloes
and all the finest spices.
You are a garden fountain,
a well of flowing water
streaming down from Lebanon.

—SONG OF SONGS 4:12–15

❧ A WIFE OF NOBLE CHARACTER

A wife of noble character who can find?
She is worth far more than rubies.
Her husband has full confidence in her
and lacks nothing of value.
She brings him good, not harm, all the days of her life.
She selects wool and flax and works with eager hands.
She is like the merchant ships,
bringing her food from afar.
She gets up while it is still dark; she provides food
for her family and portions for her servant girls.
She considers a field and buys it;
out of her earnings she plants a vineyard.
She sets about her work vigorously;
her arms are strong for her tasks.
She sees that her trading is profitable,
and her lamp does not go out at night.
In her hand she holds the distaff
and grasps the spindle with her fingers.
She opens her arms to the poor
and extends her hands to the needy.
When it snows, she has no fear for her household;
for all of them are clothed in scarlet.
She makes coverings for her bed;
she is clothed in fine linen and purple.
Her husband is respected at the city gate,
where he takes his seat among the elders of the land.

—PROVERBS 31:10–23

A WIFE OF NOBLE CHARACTER

A wife of noble character who can find?
She is worth far more than rubies.
She makes linen garments and sells them,
and supplies the merchants with sashes.
She is clothed with strength and dignity;
she can laugh at the days to come.
She speaks with wisdom,
and faithful instruction is on her tongue.
She watches over the affairs of her household
and does not eat the bread of idleness.
Her children arise and call her blessed;
her husband also, and he praises her:
"Many women do noble things,
but you surpass them all."
Charm is deceptive, and beauty is fleeting;
but a woman who fears the LORD is to be praised.
Give her the reward she has earned,
and let her works bring her praise at the city gate.

—PROVERBS 31:10, 24–31

❧ WHEN WILL YOU BECOME WISE?

Take heed, you senseless ones among the people;
you fools, when will you become wise?
Does he who implanted the ear not hear?
Does he who formed the eye not see?
Does he who disciplines nations not punish?
Does he who teaches man lack knowledge?
The LORD knows the thoughts of man;
he knows that they are futile.

—PSALM 94:8–11

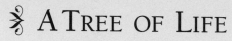 A TREE OF LIFE

Hope deferred makes the heart sick,
but a longing fulfilled is a tree of life.

—PROVERBS 13:12

WHERE MORNING DAWNS AND EVENING FADES

Those living far away fear your wonders;
where morning dawns and evening fades
you call forth songs of joy.
You care for the land and water it;
you enrich it abundantly.
The streams of God are filled with water
to provide the people with grain,
for so you have ordained it.
You drench its furrows
and level its ridges;
you soften it with showers
and bless its crops.
You crown the year with your bounty,
and your carts overflow with abundance.
The grasslands of the desert overflow;
the hills are clothed with gladness.
The meadows are covered with flocks
and the valleys are mantled with grain;
they shout for joy and sing.

—PSALM 65:8–13

WE RISE UP

Some trust in chariots and some in horses,
but we trust in the name of the LORD our God.
They are brought to their knees and fall,
but we rise up and stand firm.
O LORD, save the king!
Answer us when we call!

—PSALM 20:7–9

❧ APPLY YOUR HEART

Pay attention and listen to the sayings of the wise;
apply your heart to what I teach,
for it is pleasing when you keep them in your heart
and have all of them ready on your lips.
So that your trust may be in the LORD,
I teach you today, even you.
Have I not written thirty sayings for you,
sayings of counsel and knowledge,
teaching you true and reliable words,
so that you can give sound answers
to him who sent you?

—PROVERBS 22:17–21

HER FALL WAS ASTOUNDING

Jerusalem has sinned greatly
and so has become unclean.
All who honored her despise her,
for they have seen her nakedness;
she herself groans
and turns away.
Her filthiness clung to her skirts;
she did not consider her future.
Her fall was astounding;
there was none to comfort her.
"Look, O LORD, on my affliction,
for the enemy has triumphed."
The enemy laid hands
on all her treasures;
she saw pagan nations
enter her sanctuary—
those you had forbidden
to enter your assembly.

—LAMENTATIONS 1:8–10

❧ YOU PRESERVE MY LIFE

Though the LORD is on high, he looks upon the lowly,
but the proud he knows from afar.
Though I walk in the midst of trouble,
you preserve my life;
you stretch out your hand against the anger of my foes,
with your right hand you save me.
The LORD will fulfill his purpose for me;
your love, O LORD, endures forever—
do not abandon the works of your hands.

—PSALM 138:6–8

I'VE DONE NOTHING WRONG

"This is the way of an adulteress:
She eats and wipes her mouth
and says, 'I've done nothing wrong.'
—PROVERBS 30:20

ALL MY WAYS

O LORD, you have searched me
and you know me.
You know when I sit and when I rise;
you perceive my thoughts from afar.
You discern my going out and my lying down;
you are familiar with all my ways.
Before a word is on my tongue
you know it completely, O LORD.

—PSALM 139:1–4

HIS CASE SEEMS RIGHT

The first to present his case seems right,
till another comes forward and questions him.

—PROVERBS 18:17

WHO WILL SEE THEM?

Hear me, O God, as I voice my complaint;
protect my life from the threat of the enemy.
Hide me from the conspiracy of the wicked,
from that noisy crowd of evildoers.
They sharpen their tongues like swords
and aim their words like deadly arrows.
They shoot from ambush at the innocent man;
they shoot at him suddenly, without fear.
They encourage each other in evil plans,
they talk about hiding their snares;
they say, "Who will see them?"
They plot injustice and say,
"We have devised a perfect plan!"
Surely the mind and heart of man are cunning.

—PSALM 64:1–6

A TYRANNICAL RULER

When the righteous triumph, there is great elation;
but when the wicked rise to power, men go into hiding.
Like a roaring lion or a charging bear
is a wicked man ruling over a helpless people.
A tyrannical ruler lacks judgment,
but he who hates ill-gotten gain will enjoy a long life.

—PROVERBS 28:12, 15–16

❧ SHE LAUGHS AT HORSE AND RIDER

"The wings of the ostrich flap joyfully,
but they cannot compare with the pinions
and feathers of the stork.
She lays her eggs on the ground
and lets them warm in the sand,
unmindful that a foot may crush them,
that some wild animal may trample them.
She treats her young harshly, as if they were not hers;
she cares not that her labor was in vain,
for God did not endow her with wisdom
or give her a share of good sense.
Yet when she spreads her feathers to run,
she laughs at horse and rider.

—JOB 39:13–18

NO ROOM FOR GOD

In his arrogance the wicked man hunts down the weak,
who are caught in the schemes he devises.
He boasts of the cravings of his heart;
he blesses the greedy and reviles the LORD.
In his pride the wicked does not seek him;
in all his thoughts there is no room for God.
His ways are always prosperous;
he is haughty and your laws are far from him;
he sneers at all his enemies.

—PSALM 10:2–5

❧ A HOT-TEMPERED MAN

Do not make friends with a hot-tempered man,
do not associate with one easily angered,
or you may learn his ways
and get yourself ensnared.

—PROVERBS 22:24–25

❧ A FOOLISH SON BRINGS GRIEF TO HIS FATHER

To have a fool for a son brings grief;
there is no joy for the father of a fool.
A cheerful heart is good medicine,
but a crushed spirit dries up the bones.
A wicked man accepts a bribe in secret
to pervert the course of justice.
A discerning man keeps wisdom in view,
but a fool's eyes wander to the ends of the earth.
A foolish son brings grief to his father
and bitterness to the one who bore him.

—PROVERBS 17:21–25

THE MIGHT OF YOUR HAND

"I cry out to you, O God, but you do not answer;
I stand up, but you merely look at me.
You turn on me ruthlessly;
with the might of your hand you attack me.
You snatch me up and drive me before the wind;
you toss me about in the storm.
I know you will bring me down to death,
to the place appointed for all the living.

—JOB 30:20–23

❧ THE TEMPEST AND STORM

My heart is in anguish within me;
the terrors of death assail me.
Fear and trembling have beset me;
horror has overwhelmed me.
I said, "Oh, that I had the wings of a dove!
I would fly away and be at rest—
I would flee far away
and stay in the desert;
I would hurry to my place of shelter,
far from the tempest and storm."

—PSALM 55:4–8

❧ God Will Call the Past to Account

I know that everything God does will endure forever;
nothing can be added to it and nothing taken from it.
God does it so that men will revere him.
Whatever is has already been,
and what will be has been before;
and God will call the past to account.

—Ecclesiastes 3:14–15

I REBELLED

"The LORD is righteous,
yet I rebelled against his command.
Listen, all you peoples;
look upon my suffering.
My young men and maidens
have gone into exile.
"I called to my allies
but they betrayed me.
My priests and my elders
perished in the city
while they searched for food
to keep themselves alive.

—LAMENTATIONS 1:18–19

WHERE DOES MY HELP COME FROM?

I lift up my eyes to the hills—
where does my help come from?
My help comes from the LORD,
the Maker of heaven and earth.
He will not let your foot slip—
he who watches over you will not slumber;
indeed, he who watches over Israel
will neither slumber nor sleep.
The LORD watches over you—
the LORD is your shade at your right hand;
the sun will not harm you by day,
nor the moon by night.
The LORD will keep you from all harm—
he will watch over your life;
the LORD will watch over your coming and going
both now and forevermore.

—PSALM 121:1–8

WHAT IS MAN?

"What is man that you make so much of him,
that you give him so much attention,
that you examine him every morning
and test him every moment?
Will you never look away from me,
or let me alone even for an instant?
If I have sinned, what have I done to you,
O watcher of men?
Why have you made me your target?
Have I become a burden to you?
Why do you not pardon my offenses
and forgive my sins?
For I will soon lie down in the dust;
you will search for me, but I will be no more."

—JOB 7:17–21

❧ SING A NEW SONG

Sing joyfully to the LORD, you righteous;
it is fitting for the upright to praise him.
Praise the LORD with the harp;
make music to him on the ten-stringed lyre.
Sing to him a new song;
play skillfully, and shout for joy.
For the word of the LORD is right and true;
he is faithful in all he does.
The LORD loves righteousness and justice;
the earth is full of his unfailing love.

—PSALM 33:1–5

WHO CAN DISCOVER IT?

All this I tested by wisdom and I said,
"I am determined to be wise"—
but this was beyond me.
Whatever wisdom may be,
it is far off and most profound—
who can discover it?
So I turned my mind to understand,
to investigate and to search out wisdom
and the scheme of things and to understand
the stupidity of wickedness
and the madness of folly.

—ECCLESIASTES 7:23–25

❧ A CORRUPT THRONE

Can a corrupt throne be allied with you—
one that brings on misery by its decrees?
They band together against the righteous
and condemn the innocent to death.
But the LORD has become my fortress,
and my God the rock in whom I take refuge.
He will repay them for their sins
and destroy them for their wickedness;
the LORD our God will destroy them.

—PSALM 94:20–23

GOD WILL BLESS US

May the peoples praise you, O God;
may all the peoples praise you.
May the nations be glad and sing for joy,
for you rule the peoples justly
and guide the nations of the earth.
May the peoples praise you, O God;
may all the peoples praise you.
Then the land will yield its harvest,
and God, our God, will bless us.
God will bless us,
and all the ends of the earth will fear him.

—PSALM 67:3–7

❧ WHO CAN SAY?

Who can say, "I have kept my heart pure;
I am clean and without sin"?

—PROVERBS 20:9

THE LIGHT OF LIFE

I am under vows to you, O God;
I will present my thank offerings to you.
For you have delivered me from death
and my feet from stumbling,
that I may walk before God
in the light of life.

—PSALM 56:12–13

❧ THE SLUGGARD

The sluggard says, "There is a lion in the road,
a fierce lion roaming the streets!"
As a door turns on its hinges,
so a sluggard turns on his bed.
The sluggard buries his hand in the dish;
he is too lazy to bring it back to his mouth.
The sluggard is wiser in his own eyes
than seven men who answer discreetly.

—PROVERBS 26:13–16

❧ FULL OF TROUBLE

O LORD, the God who saves me,
day and night I cry out before you.
May my prayer come before you;
turn your ear to my cry.
For my soul is full of trouble
and my life draws near the grave.
I am counted among those who go down to the pit;
I am like a man without strength.
I am set apart with the dead,
like the slain who lie in the grave,
whom you remember no more,
who are cut off from your care.

—PSALM 88:1–5

❧ DAVID

He chose David his servant
and took him from the sheep pens;
from tending the sheep he brought him
to be the shepherd of his people Jacob,
of Israel his inheritance.
And David shepherded them with integrity of heart;
with skillful hands he led them.

—PSALM 78:70–72

A FOOL

Like cutting off one's feet or drinking violence
is the sending of a message by the hand of a fool.
Like a lame man's legs that hang limp
is a proverb in the mouth of a fool.
Like tying a stone in a sling
is the giving of honor to a fool.

—PROVERBS 26:6–8

EXAMINE MY HEART

Test me, O LORD, and try me,
examine my heart and my mind;
for your love is ever before me,
and I walk continually in your truth.
I do not sit with deceitful men,
nor do I consort with hypocrites;
I abhor the assembly of evildoers
and refuse to sit with the wicked.

—PSALM 26:2–5

SHOW RESTRAINT

Do not wear yourself out to get rich;
have the wisdom to show restraint.
Cast but a glance at riches, and they are gone,
for they will surely sprout wings
and fly off to the sky like an eagle.

—PROVERBS 23:4–5

❧ SMOOTH AS BUTTER

My companion attacks his friends;
he violates his covenant.
His speech is smooth as butter,
yet war is in his heart.

—PSALM 55:20–21

SEVEN PILLARS

Wisdom has built her house;
she has hewn out its seven pillars.
She has prepared her meat and mixed her wine;
she has also set her table.
She has sent out her maids, and she calls
from the highest point of the city.
"Let all who are simple come in here!"
she says to those who lack judgment.
"Come, eat my food
and drink the wine I have mixed.
Leave your simple ways and you will live;
walk in the way of understanding.

—PROVERBS 9:1–6

❧ IT IS YOUR LIFE

Listen, my son, accept what I say,
and the years of your life will be many.
I guide you in the way of wisdom
and lead you along straight paths.
When you walk, your steps will not be hampered;
when you run, you will not stumble.
Hold on to instruction, do not let it go;
guard it well, for it is your life.
Do not set foot on the path of the wicked
or walk in the way of evil men.
Avoid it, do not travel on it;
turn from it and go on your way.

—PROVERBS 4:10–15

FOUR THINGS

"Under three things the earth trembles,
under four it cannot bear up:
a servant who becomes king,
a fool who is full of food,
an unloved woman who is married,
and a maidservant who displaces her mistress.

—PROVERBS 30:21–23

THE STRENGTH OF MY HEART

When my heart was grieved
and my spirit embittered,
I was senseless and ignorant;
I was a brute beast before you.
Yet I am always with you;
you hold me by my right hand.
You guide me with your counsel,
and afterward you will take me into glory.
Whom have I in heaven but you?
And earth has nothing I desire besides you.
My flesh and my heart may fail,
but God is the strength of my heart
and my portion forever.

—PSALM 73:21–26

❧ WHO IS THIS?

Who is this that appears like the dawn,
fair as the moon, bright as the sun,
majestic as the stars in procession?

—SONG OF SONGS 6:10

FOUR THINGS

"Four things on earth are small,
yet they are extremely wise:
Ants are creatures of little strength,
yet they store up their food in the summer;
coneys are creatures of little power,
yet they make their home in the crags;
locusts have no king,
yet they advance together in ranks;
a lizard can be caught with the hand,
yet it is found in kings' palaces.

—PROVERBS 30:24–28

NOW I OBEY YOUR WORD

Do good to your servant
according to your word, O LORD.
Teach me knowledge and good judgment,
for I believe in your commands.
Before I was afflicted I went astray,
but now I obey your word.
You are good, and what you do is good;
teach me your decrees.
Though the arrogant have smeared me with lies,
I keep your precepts with all my heart.
Their hearts are callous and unfeeling,
but I delight in your law.
It was good for me to be afflicted
so that I might learn your decrees.
The law from your mouth is more precious to me
than thousands of pieces of silver and gold.

—PSALM 119:65–72

IF I RISE ON THE WINGS OF THE DAWN

Where can I go from your Spirit?
Where can I flee from your presence?
If I go up to the heavens, you are there;
if I make my bed in the depths, you are there.
If I rise on the wings of the dawn,
if I settle on the far side of the sea,
even there your hand will guide me,
your right hand will hold me fast.

—PSALM 139:7–10

❧ A TIME FOR EVERY DEED

And I saw something else under the sun:
In the place of judgment—wickedness was there,
in the place of justice—wickedness was there.
I thought in my heart,
"God will bring to judgment
both the righteous and the wicked,
for there will be a time for every activity,
a time for every deed."

—ECCLESIASTES 3:16–17

GOD'S FLAWLESS WORD

As for God, his way is perfect;
the word of the LORD is flawless.
He is a shield
for all who take refuge in him.
For who is God besides the LORD?
And who is the Rock except our God?
It is God who arms me with strength
and makes my way perfect.
He makes my feet like the feet of a deer;
he enables me to stand on the heights.
He trains my hands for battle;
my arms can bend a bow of bronze.
You give me your shield of victory,
and your right hand sustains me;
you stoop down to make me great.
You broaden the path beneath me,
so that my ankles do not turn.

—PSALM 18:30–36

❧ GO TO THE ANT

Go to the ant, you sluggard;
consider its ways and be wise!
It has no commander,
no overseer or ruler,
yet it stores its provisions in summer
and gathers its food at harvest.
How long will you lie there, you sluggard?
When will you get up from your sleep?
A little sleep, a little slumber,
a little folding of the hands to rest—
and poverty will come on you like a bandit
and scarcity like an armed man.

—PROVERBS 6:6–11

DOES THE EAGLE SOAR?

"Does the hawk take flight by your wisdom
and spread his wings toward the south?
Does the eagle soar at your command
and build his nest on high?
He dwells on a cliff and stays there at night;
a rocky crag is his stronghold.
From there he seeks out his food;
his eyes detect it from afar.
His young ones feast on blood,
and where the slain are, there is he."

—JOB 39:26–30

❧ MY BONES GROW WEAK

Be merciful to me, O LORD, for I am in distress;
my eyes grow weak with sorrow,
my soul and my body with grief.
My life is consumed by anguish
and my years by groaning;
my strength fails because of my affliction,
and my bones grow weak.

—PSALM 31:9–10

A MAN TORMENTED

He who conceals his sins does not prosper,
but whoever confesses and renounces them finds mercy.
A man tormented by the guilt of murder
will be a fugitive till death;
let no one support him.
He whose walk is blameless is kept safe,
but he whose ways are perverse will suddenly fall.

—PROVERBS 28:13, 17–18

❧ I WILL AWAKEN THE DAWN

My heart is steadfast, O God;
I will sing and make music with all my soul.
Awake, harp and lyre!
I will awaken the dawn.
I will praise you, O LORD, among the nations;
I will sing of you among the peoples.
For great is your love, higher than the heavens;
your faithfulness reaches to the skies.
Be exalted, O God, above the heavens,
and let your glory be over all the earth.

—PSALM 108:1–5

AS INTERMITTENT STREAMS

"A despairing man should have
the devotion of his friends,
even though he forsakes the fear of the Almighty.
But my brothers are as undependable
as intermittent streams,
as the streams that overflow
when darkened by thawing ice
and swollen with melting snow,
but that cease to flow in the dry season,
and in the heat vanish from their channels.

—JOB 6:14–17

"My Foot Is Slipping"

Who will rise up for me against the wicked?
Who will take a stand for me against evildoers?
Unless the LORD had given me help,
I would soon have dwelt in the silence of death.
When I said, "My foot is slipping,"
your love, O LORD, supported me.
When anxiety was great within me,
your consolation brought joy to my soul.

—PSALM 94:16–19

AUGUST 14

 # SHE WILL ENSNARE

I find more bitter than death
the woman who is a snare,
whose heart is a trap
and whose hands are chains.
The man who pleases God will escape her,
but the sinner she will ensnare.

—ECCLESIASTES 7:26

I CALL TO GOD

But I call to God,
and the LORD saves me.
Evening, morning and noon
I cry out in distress,
and he hears my voice.
He ransoms me unharmed
from the battle waged against me,
even though many oppose me.
God, who is enthroned forever,
will hear them and afflict them—
men who never change their ways
and have no fear of God.

—PSALM 55:16–19

A FOOL REPEATS HIS FOLLY

Like a thornbush in a drunkard's hand
is a proverb in the mouth of a fool.
Like an archer who wounds at random
is he who hires a fool or any passer-by.
As a dog returns to its vomit,
so a fool repeats his folly.
Do you see a man wise in his own eyes?
There is more hope for a fool than for him.

—PROVERBS 26:9–12

FORGET NOT ALL HIS BENEFITS

Praise the LORD, O my soul,
and forget not all his benefits—
who forgives all your sins
and heals all your diseases,
who redeems your life from the pit
and crowns you with love and compassion,
who satisfies your desires with good things
so that your youth is renewed like the eagle's.

—PSALM 103:2–5

AUGUST 18

❧ LEAN NOT ON YOUR OWN UNDERSTANDING

*Trust in the LORD with all your heart
and lean not on your own understanding;
in all your ways acknowledge him,
and he will make your paths straight.*

—PROVERBS 3:5–6

❧ By the Word of the Lord

By the word of the LORD were the heavens made,
their starry host by the breath of his mouth.
He gathers the waters of the sea into jars;
he puts the deep into storehouses.
Let all the earth fear the LORD;
let all the people of the world revere him.
For he spoke, and it came to be;
he commanded, and it stood firm.
The LORD foils the plans of the nations;
he thwarts the purposes of the peoples.
But the plans of the LORD stand firm forever,
the purposes of his heart through all generations.

—PSALM 33:6–11

OLDEN DAYS

Do not say,
"Why were the old days better than these?"
For it is not wise to ask such questions.

—ECCLESIASTES 7:10

A BLAMELESS HEART

I will sing of your love and justice;
to you, O LORD, I will sing praise.
I will be careful to lead a blameless life—
when will you come to me?
I will walk in my house with blameless heart.
I will set before my eyes no vile thing.
The deeds of faithless men I hate;
they will not cling to me.
Men of perverse heart shall be far from me;
I will have nothing to do with evil.

—PSALM 101:1–4

THE GLORY OF GOD

The heavens declare the glory of God;
the skies proclaim the work of his hands.
Day after day they pour forth speech;
night after night they display knowledge.
There is no speech or language
where their voice is not heard.
Their voice goes out into all the earth,
their words to the ends of the world.

—PSALM 19:1–4

❧ THE POOR

The poor are shunned even by their neighbors,
but the rich have many friends.
He who despises his neighbor sins,
but blessed is he who is kind to the needy.
He who oppresses the poor
shows contempt for their Maker,
but whoever is kind to the needy honors God.

—PROVERBS 14:20, 21, 31

I CALL TO YOU EVERY DAY

My eyes are dim with grief.
I call to you, O LORD, every day;
I spread out my hands to you.
Do you show your wonders to the dead?
Do those who are dead rise up and praise you?
Is your love declared in the grave,
your faithfulness in Destruction?
Are your wonders known in the place of darkness,
or your righteous deeds in the land of oblivion?
But I cry to you for help, O LORD;
in the morning my prayer comes before you.

—PSALM 88:9–13

❧ CHASING FANTASIES

He who works his land will have abundant food,
but he who chases fantasies lacks judgment.

—PROVERBS 12:11

I LOVE YOUR LAW

Oh, how I love your law!
I meditate on it all day long.
Your commands make me wiser than my enemies,
for they are ever with me.
I have more insight than all my teachers,
for I meditate on your statutes.
I have more understanding than the elders,
for I obey your precepts.
I have kept my feet from every evil path
so that I might obey your word.
I have not departed from your laws,
for you yourself have taught me.
How sweet are your words to my taste,
sweeter than honey to my mouth!
I gain understanding from your precepts;
therefore I hate every wrong path.

—PSALM 119:97–104

IN THE MORNING

Give ear to my words, O LORD,
consider my sighing.
Listen to my cry for help,
my King and my God,
for to you I pray.
In the morning, O LORD, you hear my voice;
in the morning I lay my requests before you
and wait in expectation.

—PSALM 5:1–3

SONGS OF JOY

You answer us with awesome deeds of righteousness,
O God our Savior,
the hope of all the ends of the earth
and of the farthest seas,
who formed the mountains by your power,
having armed yourself with strength,
who stilled the roaring of the seas,
the roaring of their waves, and the turmoil of the nations.
Those living far away fear your wonders;
where morning dawns and evening fades
you call forth songs of joy.

—PSALM 65:5–8

I REMEMBER YOUR ANCIENT LAWS

Remember your word to your servant,
for you have given me hope.
My comfort in my suffering is this:
Your promise preserves my life.
The arrogant mock me without restraint,
but I do not turn from your law.
I remember your ancient laws, O LORD,
and I find comfort in them.
Indignation grips me because of the wicked,
who have forsaken your law.
Your decrees are the theme of my song
wherever I lodge.
In the night I remember your name, O LORD,
and I will keep your law.
This has been my practice:
I obey your precepts.

—PSALM 119:49–56

WHEN I HOPED FOR GOOD, EVIL CAME

"Surely no one lays a hand on a broken man
when he cries for help in his distress.
Have I not wept for those in trouble?
Has not my soul grieved for the poor?
Yet when I hoped for good, evil came;
when I looked for light, then came darkness.
The churning inside me never stops;
days of suffering confront me.
I go about blackened, but not by the sun;
I stand up in the assembly and cry for help.
I have become a brother of jackals,
a companion of owls.
My skin grows black and peels;
my body burns with fever.
My harp is tuned to mourning,
and my flute to the sound of wailing.

—JOB 30:24–31

⅋ TWO THINGS

Lowborn men are but a breath,
the highborn are but a lie;
if weighed on a balance, they are nothing;
together they are only a breath.
Do not trust in extortion
or take pride in stolen goods;
though your riches increase,
do not set your heart on them.
One thing God has spoken,
two things have I heard:
that you, O God, are strong,
and that you, O Lord, are loving.
Surely you will reward each person
according to what he has done.

—PSALM 62:9–12

❧ GREAT REWARD

The law of the LORD is perfect,
reviving the soul.
The statutes of the LORD are trustworthy,
making wise the simple.
The precepts of the LORD are right,
giving joy to the heart.
The commands of the LORD are radiant,
giving light to the eyes.
The fear of the LORD is pure,
enduring forever.
The ordinances of the LORD are sure
and altogether righteous.
They are more precious than gold,
than much pure gold;
they are sweeter than honey,
than honey from the comb.
By them is your servant warned;
in keeping them there is great reward.

—PSALM 19:7–11

THEY SCOFFED

The visions of your prophets
were false and worthless;
they did not expose your sin
to ward off your captivity.
The oracles they gave you
were false and misleading.
All who pass your way
clap their hands at you;
they scoff and shake their heads
at the Daughter of Jerusalem:
"Is this the city that was called
the perfection of beauty,
the joy of the whole earth?"
All your enemies open their mouths
wide against you;
they scoff and gnash their teeth
and say, "We have swallowed her up.
This is the day we have waited for;
we have lived to see it."

—LAMENTATIONS 2:14–16

I WILL EXPOUND MY RIDDLE

Hear this, all you peoples;
listen, all who live in this world,
both low and high,
rich and poor alike:
My mouth will speak words of wisdom;
the utterance from my heart will give understanding.
I will turn my ear to a proverb;
with the harp I will expound my riddle:

—PSALM 49:1–4

A Man Lacking Judgment

Men do not despise a thief if he steals
to satisfy his hunger when he is starving.
Yet if he is caught, he must pay sevenfold,
though it costs him all the wealth of his house.
But a man who commits adultery lacks judgment;
whoever does so destroys himself.
Blows and disgrace are his lot,
and his shame will never be wiped away;
for jealousy arouses a husband's fury,
and he will show no mercy when he takes revenge.
He will not accept any compensation;
he will refuse the bribe, however great it is.

—Proverbs 6:30–35

ITS BUILDERS LABOR IN VAIN

Unless the LORD builds the house,
its builders labor in vain.
Unless the LORD watches over the city,
the watchmen stand guard in vain.
In vain you rise early
and stay up late,
toiling for food to eat—
for he grants sleep to those he loves.

—PSALM 127:1–2

❧ THE YOUNG MEN HAVE STOPPED THEIR MUSIC

The elders are gone from the city gate;
the young men have stopped their music.
Joy is gone from our hearts;
our dancing has turned to mourning.
The crown has fallen from our head.
Woe to us, for we have sinned!
Because of this our hearts are faint,
because of these things our eyes grow dim
for Mount Zion, which lies desolate,
with jackals prowling over it.

—LAMENTATIONS 5:14–18

❧ A KING CANNOT SAVE

No king is saved by the size of his army;
no warrior escapes by his great strength.
A horse is a vain hope for deliverance;
despite all its great strength it cannot save.
But the eyes of the LORD are on those who fear him,
on those whose hope is in his unfailing love,
to deliver them from death
and keep them alive in famine.

—PSALM 33:16–19

⸙ TWO ARE BETTER THAN ONE

Two are better than one,
because they have a good return for their work:
If one falls down,
his friend can help him up.
But pity the man who falls
and has no one to help him up!
Also, if two lie down together, they will keep warm.
But how can one keep warm alone?
Though one may be overpowered,
two can defend themselves.
A cord of three strands is not quickly broken.

—ECCLESIASTES 4:9–12

THE FAITHFUL IN THE LAND

My eyes will be on the faithful in the land,
that they may dwell with me;
he whose walk is blameless
will minister to me.
No one who practices deceit
will dwell in my house;
no one who speaks falsely
will stand in my presence.

—PSALM 101:6–7

SPEAK UP

"Speak up for those who cannot speak for themselves,
for the rights of all who are destitute.
Speak up and judge fairly;
defend the rights of the poor and needy."

—PROVERBS 31:8–9

❧ EVEN THOUGH I WALK

The LORD is my shepherd,
I shall not be in want.
He makes me lie down in green pastures,
he leads me beside quiet waters,
he restores my soul.
He guides me in paths of righteousness
for his name's sake.
Even though I walk
through the valley of the shadow of death,
I will fear no evil, for you are with me;
your rod and your staff, they comfort me.
You prepare a table before me
in the presence of my enemies.
You anoint my head with oil; my cup overflows.
Surely goodness and love will follow me
all the days of my life,
and I will dwell in the house of the LORD forever.

—PSALM 23:1–6

SEPTEMBER 12

❧ CHILDREN FAINT IN THE STREETS OF THE CITY

My eyes fail from weeping,
I am in torment within,
my heart is poured out on the ground
because my people are destroyed,
because children and infants faint
in the streets of the city.
They say to their mothers,
"Where is bread and wine?"
as they faint like wounded men
in the streets of the city,
as their lives ebb away
in their mothers' arms.
What can I say for you?
With what can I compare you,
O Daughter of Jerusalem?
To what can I liken you,
that I may comfort you,
O Virgin Daughter of Zion?
Your wound is as deep as the sea.
Who can heal you?

—LAMENTATIONS 2:11–13

❧ HE WILL SHOW COMPASSION

For men are not cast off by the Lord forever.
Though he brings grief, he will show compassion,
so great is his unfailing love.
For he does not willingly bring affliction
or grief to the children of men.

To crush underfoot all prisoners in the land,
to deny a man his rights before the Most High,
to deprive a man of justice—
would not the Lord see such things?

—LAMENTATIONS 3:31–36

BECAUSE HE LOVES ME

"Because he loves me," says the LORD,
"I will rescue him; I will protect him,
for he acknowledges my name.
He will call upon me, and I will answer him;
I will be with him in trouble,
I will deliver him and honor him.
With long life will I satisfy him
and show him my salvation."

—PSALM 91:14–16

❧ A WISE SON

Listen to your father, who gave you life,
and do not despise your mother when she is old.
Buy the truth and do not sell it;
get wisdom, discipline and understanding.
The father of a righteous man has great joy;
he who has a wise son delights in him.
May your father and mother be glad;
may she who gave you birth rejoice!

—PROVERBS 23:22–25

❧ I Am Your Servant

*Precious in the sight of the L*ORD
is the death of his saints.
*O L*ORD, *truly I am your servant;*
I am your servant, the son of your maidservant;
you have freed me from my chains.

—PSALM 116:15–16

WHEN GOD CONFRONTS ME

"If I have denied justice
to my menservants and maidservants
when they had a grievance against me,
what will I do when God confronts me?
What will I answer when called to account?
Did not he who made me in the womb make them?
Did not the same one form us both within our mothers?

—JOB 31:13–15

COME IN HERE!

The woman Folly is loud;
she is undisciplined and without knowledge.
She sits at the door of her house,
on a seat at the highest point of the city,
calling out to those who pass by,
who go straight on their way.
"Let all who are simple come in here!"
she says to those who lack judgment.
"Stolen water is sweet;
food eaten in secret is delicious!"
But little do they know that the dead are there,
that her guests are in the depths of the grave.

—PROVERBS 9:13–18

❧ I Am Distraught

Listen to my prayer, O God,
do not ignore my plea;
hear me and answer me.
My thoughts trouble me and I am distraught
at the voice of the enemy,
at the stares of the wicked;
for they bring down suffering upon me
and revile me in their anger.

—PSALM 55:1–3

FOUR THINGS

"There are three things that are stately in their stride,
four that move with stately bearing:
a lion, mighty among beasts,
who retreats before nothing;
a strutting rooster, a he-goat,
and a king with his army around him.

—PROVERBS 30:29–31

❧ YOUR CREATURES

How many are your works, O LORD!
In wisdom you made them all;
the earth is full of your creatures.
There is the sea, vast and spacious,
teeming with creatures beyond number—
living things both large and small.
There the ships go to and fro,
and the leviathan, which you formed to frolic there.

—PSALM 104:24–26

SEPTEMBER 22

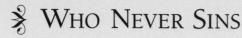 # WHO NEVER SINS

There is not a righteous man on earth
who does what is right and never sins.

—ECCLESIASTES 7:20

❧ LIKE EAGLES SWOOPING DOWN

"My days are swifter than a runner;
they fly away without a glimpse of joy.
They skim past like boats of papyrus,
like eagles swooping down on their prey.

—JOB 9:25–26

❧ ETERNAL PRAISE

*The fear of the LORD is the beginning of wisdom;
all who follow his precepts have good understanding.
To him belongs eternal praise.*

—PSALM 111:10

 # THE BUYER

"It's no good, it's no good!" says the buyer;
then off he goes and boasts about his purchase.

—PROVERBS 20:14

WAIT FOR THE LORD

Though my father and mother forsake me,
the LORD will receive me.
Teach me your way, O LORD;
lead me in a straight path
because of my oppressors.
Do not turn me over to the desire of my foes,
for false witnesses rise up against me,
breathing out violence.
I am still confident of this:
I will see the goodness of the LORD
in the land of the living.
Wait for the LORD;
be strong and take heart
and wait for the LORD.

—PSALM 27:10–14

❧ ZEAL WITHOUT KNOWLEDGE

It is not good to have zeal without knowledge,
nor to be hasty and miss the way.

—PROVERBS 19:2

WISDOM BRIGHTENS

Who is like the wise man?
Who knows the explanation of things?
Wisdom brightens a man's face
and changes its hard appearance.

—ECCLESIASTES 8:1

❧ A MALICIOUS MAN

Like a coating of glaze over earthenware
are fervent lips with an evil heart.
A malicious man disguises himself with his lips,
but in his heart he harbors deceit.
Though his speech is charming, do not believe him,
for seven abominations fill his heart.

—PROVERBS 26:23–25

❧ JOY TO HIS FATHER

A man who loves wisdom brings joy to his father,
but a companion of prostitutes squanders his wealth.

—PROVERBS 29:3

❧ GREAT IS YOUR FAITHFULNESS

I remember my affliction and my wandering,
the bitterness and the gall.
I well remember them,
and my soul is downcast within me.
Yet this I call to mind
and therefore I have hope:

Because of the LORD'S great love
we are not consumed,
for his compassions never fail.
They are new every morning;
great is your faithfulness.
I say to myself, "The LORD is my portion;
therefore I will wait for him."
—LAMENTATIONS 3:19–24

MY SOUL THIRSTS FOR GOD

As the deer pants for streams of water,
so my soul pants for you, O God.
My soul thirsts for God, for the living God.
When can I go and meet with God?
My tears have been my food
day and night,
while men say to me all day long,
"Where is your God?"
These things I remember
as I pour out my soul:
how I used to go with the multitude,
leading the procession to the house of God,
with shouts of joy and thanksgiving
among the festive throng.

—PSALM 42:1–4

❧ SHE LIES IN WAIT

My son, give me your heart
and let your eyes keep to my ways,
for a prostitute is a deep pit
and a wayward wife is a narrow well.
Like a bandit she lies in wait,
and multiplies the unfaithful among men.

—PROVERBS 23:26–28

❧ HE IS MY ROCK

The righteous will flourish like a palm tree,
they will grow like a cedar of Lebanon;
planted in the house of the LORD,
they will flourish in the courts of our God.
They will still bear fruit in old age,
they will stay fresh and green,
proclaiming, "The LORD is upright;
he is my Rock, and there is no wickedness in him."

—PSALM 92:12–15

❧ HE INSTRUCTS SINNERS

Good and upright is the LORD;
therefore he instructs sinners in his ways.
He guides the humble in what is right
and teaches them his way.
All the ways of the LORD are loving and faithful
for those who keep the demands of his covenant.

—PSALM 25:8–10

THROUGH ALL GENERATIONS

The mountains will bring prosperity to the people,
the hills the fruit of righteousness.
He will defend the afflicted among the people
and save the children of the needy;
he will crush the oppressor.
He will endure as long as the sun,
as long as the moon, through all generations.
He will be like rain falling on a mown field,
like showers watering the earth.
In his days the righteous will flourish;
prosperity will abound till the moon is no more.

—PSALM 72:3–7

❧ BOLD AS A LION

The wicked man flees though no one pursues,
but the righteous are as bold as a lion.

—PROVERBS 28:1

HERE I AM

Then I said, "Here I am, I have come—
it is written about me in the scroll.
I desire to do your will, O my God;
your law is within my heart."
I proclaim righteousness in the great assembly;
I do not seal my lips,
as you know, O LORD.
I do not hide your righteousness in my heart;
I speak of your faithfulness and salvation.
I do not conceal your love and your truth
from the great assembly.

—PSALM 40:7–10

❧ THE CLOUDS LET DROP THE DEW

By wisdom the LORD laid the earth's foundations,
by understanding he set the heavens in place;
by his knowledge the deeps were divided,
and the clouds let drop the dew.

—PROVERBS 3:19–20

HOW I HATED DISCIPLINE!

At the end of your life you will groan,
when your flesh and body are spent.
You will say, "How I hated discipline!
How my heart spurned correction!
I would not obey my teachers
or listen to my instructors.
I have come to the brink of utter ruin
in the midst of the whole assembly."

—PROVERBS 5:11–14

SOME WANDERED IN DESERT WASTELANDS

Let the redeemed of the LORD say this—
those he redeemed from the hand of the foe,
those he gathered from the lands,
from east and west, from north and south.
Some wandered in desert wastelands,
finding no way to a city where they could settle.
They were hungry and thirsty,
and their lives ebbed away.
Then they cried out to the LORD in their trouble,
and he delivered them from their distress.
He led them by a straight way
to a city where they could settle.
Let them give thanks to the LORD for his unfailing love
and his wonderful deeds for men,
for he satisfies the thirsty
and fills the hungry with good things.

—PSALM 107:2–9

HIS FAITHFULNESS

For the LORD gives wisdom,
and from his mouth come knowledge and understanding.
He holds victory in store for the upright,
he is a shield to those whose walk is blameless,
for he guards the course of the just
and protects the way of his faithful ones.
Then you will understand what is right and just
and fair—every good path.
For wisdom will enter your heart,
and knowledge will be pleasant to your soul.
Discretion will protect you,
and understanding will guard you.

—PROVERBS 2:6–11

❧ A LIGHT FOR MY PATH

Your word is a lamp to my feet
and a light for my path.
I have taken an oath and confirmed it,
that I will follow your righteous laws.
I have suffered much;
preserve my life, O LORD, according to your word.
Accept, O LORD, the willing praise of my mouth,
and teach me your laws.
Though I constantly take my life in my hands,
I will not forget your law.
The wicked have set a snare for me,
but I have not strayed from your precepts.
Your statutes are my heritage forever;
they are the joy of my heart.
My heart is set on keeping your decrees to the very end.

—PSALM 119:105–112

ANGER PRODUCES STRIFE

"If you have played the fool and exalted yourself,
or if you have planned evil,
clap your hand over your mouth!
For as churning the milk produces butter,
and as twisting the nose produces blood,
so stirring up anger produces strife."

—PROVERBS 30:32–33

❧ LIKE THE BEASTS THAT PERISH

For all can see that wise men die;
the foolish and the senseless alike perish
and leave their wealth to others.
Their tombs will remain their houses forever,
their dwellings for endless generations,
though they had named lands after themselves.
But man, despite his riches, does not endure;
he is like the beasts that perish.

—PSALM 49:10–12

❧ A QUARREL

Starting a quarrel is like breaching a dam;
so drop the matter before a dispute breaks out.
He who loves a quarrel loves sin;
he who builds a high gate invites destruction.

—PROVERBS 17:14, 19

❧ FROM ALL ETERNITY

The LORD reigns, he is robed in majesty;
the LORD is robed in majesty
and is armed with strength.
The world is firmly established;
it cannot be moved.
Your throne was established long ago;
you are from all eternity.
The seas have lifted up, O LORD,
the seas have lifted up their voice;
the seas have lifted up their pounding waves.
Mightier than the thunder of the great waters,
mightier than the breakers of the sea—
the LORD on high is mighty.
Your statutes stand firm;
holiness adorns your house
for endless days, O LORD.

—PSALM 93:1–5

His Heart Is Secure

Even in darkness light dawns for the upright,
for the gracious and compassionate and righteous man.
Good will come to him who is generous and lends freely,
who conducts his affairs with justice.
Surely he will never be shaken;
a righteous man will be remembered forever.
He will have no fear of bad news;
his heart is steadfast, trusting in the LORD.
His heart is secure, he will have no fear;
in the end he will look in triumph on his foes.
He has scattered abroad his gifts to the poor,
his righteousness endures forever;
his horn will be lifted high in honor.

—Psalm 112:4–9

❧ WHAT IS MAN?

When I consider your heavens,
the work of your fingers,
the moon and the stars,
which you have set in place,
what is man that you are mindful of him,
the son of man that you care for him?
You made him a little lower than the heavenly beings
and crowned him with glory and honor.

—PSALM 8:3–5

YOU WILL REMEMBER THE STRUGGLE

*"Can you pull in the leviathan with a fishhook
or tie down his tongue with a rope?
Can you put a cord through his nose
or pierce his jaw with a hook?
Will he keep begging you for mercy?
Will he speak to you with gentle words?
Will he make an agreement with you
for you to take him as your slave for life?
Can you make a pet of him like a bird
or put him on a leash for your girls?
Will traders barter for him?
Will they divide him up among the merchants?
Can you fill his hide with harpoons
or his head with fishing spears?
If you lay a hand on him,
you will remember the struggle and never do it again!
Any hope of subduing him is false;
the mere sight of him is overpowering.
No one is fierce enough to rouse him.
Who then is able to stand against me?
Who has a claim against me that I must pay?
Everything under heaven belongs to me.*

—JOB 41:1–11

HE DEFIES ALL SOUND JUDGMENT

An unfriendly man pursues selfish ends;
he defies all sound judgment.
A fool finds no pleasure in understanding
but delights in airing his own opinions.
When wickedness comes, so does contempt,
and with shame comes disgrace.
The words of a man's mouth are deep waters,
but the fountain of wisdom is a bubbling brook.
It is not good to be partial to the wicked
or to deprive the innocent of justice.
A fool's lips bring him strife,
and his mouth invites a beating.
A fool's mouth is his undoing,
and his lips are a snare to his soul.
The words of a gossip are like choice morsels;
they go down to a man's inmost parts.

—PROVERBS 18:1–8

IT IS THE SPIRIT IN A MAN

So Elihu son of Barakel the Buzite said:
"I am young in years, and you are old;
that is why I was fearful,
not daring to tell you what I know.
I thought, 'Age should speak;
advanced years should teach wisdom.'
But it is the spirit in a man,
the breath of the Almighty,
that gives him understanding.
It is not only the old who are wise,
not only the aged who understand what is right.

—JOB 32:6–9

❧ WHERE IS THEIR GOD?

Why do the nations say,
"Where is their God?"
Our God is in heaven;
he does whatever pleases him.
But their idols are silver and gold,
made by the hands of men.
They have mouths, but cannot speak,
eyes, but they cannot see;
they have ears, but cannot hear,
noses, but they cannot smell;
they have hands, but cannot feel,
feet, but they cannot walk;
nor can they utter a sound with their throats.
Those who make them will be like them,
and so will all who trust in them.

—PSALM 115:2–8

NONE TO COMFORT HER

How deserted lies the city,
once so full of people!
How like a widow is she,
who once was great among the nations!
She who was queen among the provinces
has now become a slave.

Bitterly she weeps at night,
tears are upon her cheeks.
Among all her lovers
there is none to comfort her.
All her friends have betrayed her;
they have become her enemies.

—LAMENTATIONS 1:1–2

❧ A New Song

I waited patiently for the LORD;
he turned to me and heard my cry.
He lifted me out of the slimy pit,
out of the mud and mire;
he set my feet on a rock
and gave me a firm place to stand.
He put a new song in my mouth,
a hymn of praise to our God.
Many will see and fear
and put their trust in the LORD.

—Psalm 40:1–3

❧ POWER OVER THE WIND

No man has power over the wind to contain it;
so no one has power over the day of his death.
As no one is discharged in time of war,
so wickedness will not release those who practice it.

—ECCLESIASTES 8:8

AN OBJECT OF SCORN

But you, O Sovereign LORD,
deal well with me for your name's sake;
out of the goodness of your love, deliver me.
For I am poor and needy,
and my heart is wounded within me.
I fade away like an evening shadow;
I am shaken off like a locust.
My knees give way from fasting;
my body is thin and gaunt.
I am an object of scorn to my accusers;
when they see me, they shake their heads.

—PSALM 109:21–25

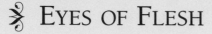 EYES OF FLESH

Do you have eyes of flesh?
Do you see as a mortal sees?
Are your days like those of a mortal
or your years like those of a man,
that you must search out my faults
and probe after my sin—
though you know that I am not guilty
and that no one can rescue me from your hand?

—JOB 10:4–7

THE MOUNTAINS QUAKE

God is our refuge and strength,
an ever-present help in trouble.
Therefore we will not fear, though the earth give way
and the mountains fall into the heart of the sea,
though its waters roar and foam
and the mountains quake with their surging.

—PSALM 46:1–3

TOMORROW

Do not boast about tomorrow,
for you do not know what a day may bring forth.

—PROVERBS 27:1

LET YOUR WORDS BE FEW

Do not be quick with your mouth,
do not be hasty in your heart
to utter anything before God.
God is in heaven
and you are on earth,
so let your words be few.
As a dream comes when there are many cares,
so the speech of a fool when there are many words.

—ECCLESIASTES 5:2–3

❧ FIRST GLEAM OF DAWN

The path of the righteous is like the first gleam of dawn,
shining ever brighter till the full light of day.
But the way of the wicked is like deep darkness;
they do not know what makes them stumble.

—PROVERBS 4:18–19

A Sun and a Shield

Better is one day in your courts
than a thousand elsewhere;
I would rather be a doorkeeper in the house of my God
than dwell in the tents of the wicked.
For the LORD God is a sun and shield;
the LORD bestows favor and honor;
no good thing does he withhold
from those whose walk is blameless.
O LORD Almighty,
blessed is the man who trusts in you.

—PSALM 84:10–12

MY EYES HAVE SEEN YOU

Then Job replied to the LORD:
"I know that you can do all things;
no plan of yours can be thwarted.
You asked, 'Who is this that obscures my counsel
without knowledge?'
Surely I spoke of things I did not understand,
things too wonderful for me to know.
"You said, 'Listen now, and I will speak;
I will question you,
and you shall answer me.'
My ears had heard of you
but now my eyes have seen you.
Therefore I despise myself
and repent in dust and ashes."

—JOB 42:1–6

PRAISE THE LORD

The highest heavens belong to the LORD,
but the earth he has given to man.
It is not the dead who praise the LORD,
those who go down to silence;
it is we who extol the LORD,
both now and forevermore.
Praise the LORD.

—PSALM 115:16–18

❊ DISCIPLINE YOUR SON

The rod of correction imparts wisdom,
but a child left to himself disgraces his mother.
Discipline your son, and he will give you peace;
he will bring delight to your soul.

—PROVERBS 29:15, 17

❧ RICHES WITHOUT UNDERSTANDING

Do not be overawed when a man grows rich,
when the splendor of his house increases;
for he will take nothing with him when he dies,
his splendor will not descend with him.
Though while he lived he counted himself blessed—
and men praise you when you prosper—
he will join the generation of his fathers,
who will never see the light of life.
A man who has riches without understanding
is like the beasts that perish.

—PSALM 49:16–20

❧ GOD DOES SPEAK

For God does speak—now one way, now another—
though man may not perceive it.
In a dream, in a vision of the night,
when deep sleep falls on men
as they slumber in their beds,
he may speak in their ears
and terrify them with warnings,
to turn man from wrongdoing
and keep him from pride,
to preserve his soul from the pit,
his life from perishing by the sword.

—JOB 33:14–18

❧ YOU LOVED THEM

We have heard with our ears, O God;
our fathers have told us
what you did in their days,
in days long ago.
With your hand you drove out the nations
and planted our fathers;
you crushed the peoples
and made our fathers flourish.
It was not by their sword that they won the land,
nor did their arm bring them victory;
it was your right hand, your arm,
and the light of your face, for you loved them.

—PSALM 44:1–3

❧ VIOLENCE AND STRIFE IN THE CITY

Confuse the wicked, O Lord, confound their speech,
for I see violence and strife in the city.
Day and night they prowl about on its walls;
malice and abuse are within it.
Destructive forces are at work in the city;
threats and lies never leave its streets.

—PSALM 55:9–11

ALL THAT GOD HAS DONE

When I applied my mind to know wisdom
and to observe man's labor on earth—
his eyes not seeing sleep day or night—
then I saw all that God has done.
No one can comprehend what goes on under the sun.
Despite all his efforts to search it out,
man cannot discover its meaning.
Even if a wise man claims he knows,
he cannot really comprehend it.

—ECCLESIASTES 8:16–17

❧ CALL UPON ME

Sacrifice thank offerings to God,
fulfill your vows to the Most High,
and call upon me in the day of trouble;
I will deliver you, and you will honor me.

—PSALM 50:14–15

YOU ARE MY SISTER

My son, keep my words
and store up my commands within you.
Keep my commands and you will live;
guard my teachings as the apple of your eye.
Bind them on your fingers;
write them on the tablet of your heart.
Say to wisdom, "You are my sister,"
and call understanding your kinsman;
they will keep you from the adulteress,
from the wayward wife with her seductive words.

—PROVERBS 7:1–5

TROUBLE IS NEAR

Yet you brought me out of the womb;
you made me trust in you
even at my mother's breast.
From birth I was cast upon you;
from my mother's womb you have been my God.
Do not be far from me,
for trouble is near
and there is no one to help.

—PSALM 22:9–11

WOE TO ME

If I sinned, you would be watching me
and would not let my offense go unpunished.
If I am guilty—woe to me!
Even if I am innocent, I cannot lift my head,
for I am full of shame
and drowned in my affliction.
If I hold my head high, you stalk me like a lion
and again display your awesome power against me.

—JOB 10:14–16

❧ CONTROLLED BY BIT AND BRIDLE

I will instruct you and teach you
in the way you should go;
I will counsel you and watch over you.
Do not be like the horse or the mule,
which have no understanding
but must be controlled by bit and bridle
or they will not come to you.
Many are the woes of the wicked,
but the LORD's unfailing love
surrounds the man who trusts in him.
Rejoice in the LORD and be glad, you righteous;
sing, all you who are upright in heart!

—PSALM 32:8–11

IN FULL VIEW

For a man's ways are in full view of the LORD,
and he examines all his paths.
The evil deeds of a wicked man ensnare him;
the cords of his sin hold him fast.
He will die for lack of discipline,
led astray by his own great folly.

—PROVERBS 5:21–23

SHOUTS OF JOY

For he remembered his holy promise
given to his servant Abraham.
He brought out his people with rejoicing,
his chosen ones with shouts of joy;
he gave them the lands of the nations,
and they fell heir to what others had toiled for—
that they might keep his precepts and observe his laws.

—PSALM 105:42–45

MAY THE NAME OF THE LORD BE PRAISED

At this, Job got up and tore his robe
and shaved his head.
Then he fell to the ground in worship and said:
"Naked I came from my mother's womb,
and naked I will depart.
The LORD gave and the LORD has taken away;
may the name of the LORD be praised."
In all this, Job did not sin by charging
God with wrongdoing.

—JOB 1:20–22

❧ FOR HE COMES

Say among the nations, "The LORD reigns."
The world is firmly established, it cannot be moved;
he will judge the peoples with equity.
Let the heavens rejoice, let the earth be glad;
let the sea resound, and all that is in it;
let the fields be jubilant, and everything in them.
Then all the trees of the forest will sing for joy;
they will sing before the LORD, for he comes,
he comes to judge the earth.
He will judge the world in righteousness
and the peoples in his truth.

—PSALM 96:10–13

❧ For Their Feet Rush into Sin

My son, if sinners entice you,
do not give in to them.
If they say, "Come along with us;
let's lie in wait for someone's blood,
let's waylay some harmless soul;
let's swallow them alive, like the grave,
and whole, like those who go down to the pit;
we will get all sorts of valuable things
and fill our houses with plunder;
throw in your lot with us,
and we will share a common purse"—
my son, do not go along with them,
do not set foot on their paths;
for their feet rush into sin,
they are swift to shed blood.

—Proverbs 1:10–16

YOUR SLEEP WILL BE SWEET

My son, preserve sound judgment and discernment,
do not let them out of your sight;
they will be life for you,
an ornament to grace your neck.
Then you will go on your way in safety,
and your foot will not stumble;
when you lie down, you will not be afraid;
when you lie down, your sleep will be sweet.
Have no fear of sudden disaster
or of the ruin that overtakes the wicked,
for the LORD will be your confidence
and will keep your foot from being snared.

—PROVERBS 3:21–26

THEY WALK IN HIS WAYS

Blessed are they whose ways are blameless,
who walk according to the law of the LORD.
Blessed are they who keep his statutes
and seek him with all their heart.
They do nothing wrong;
they walk in his ways.

—PSALM 119:1–3

❧ BUT IT HAPPENED

The kings of the earth did not believe,
nor did any of the world's people,
that enemies and foes could enter
the gates of Jerusalem.
But it happened because of the sins of her prophets
and the iniquities of her priests,
who shed within her
the blood of the righteous.

—LAMENTATIONS 4:12–13

FULFILL YOUR VOW

When you make a vow to God,
do not delay in fulfilling it.
He has no pleasure in fools; fulfill your vow.
It is better not to vow
than to make a vow and not fulfill it.
Do not let your mouth lead you into sin.
And do not protest to the temple messenger,
"My vow was a mistake."
Why should God be angry at what you say
and destroy the work of your hands?
Much dreaming and many words are meaningless.
Therefore stand in awe of God.

—ECCLESIASTES 5:4–7

❧ But I Am Not Hurt!

Who has woe? Who has sorrow?
Who has strife? Who has complaints?
Who has needless bruises?
Who has bloodshot eyes?
Those who linger over wine,
who go to sample bowls of mixed wine.
Do not gaze at wine when it is red,
when it sparkles in the cup,
when it goes down smoothly!
In the end it bites like a snake
and poisons like a viper.
Your eyes will see strange sights
and your mind imagine confusing things.
You will be like one sleeping on the high seas,
lying on top of the rigging.
"They hit me," you will say, "but I'm not hurt!
They beat me, but I don't feel it!
When will I wake up
so I can find another drink?"

—Proverbs 23:29–35

MEN OF THIS WORLD

Rise up, O LORD, confront them, bring them down;
rescue me from the wicked by your sword.
O LORD, by your hand save me from such men,
from men of this world whose reward is in this life.
You still the hunger of those you cherish;
their sons have plenty,
and they store up wealth for their children.
And I—in righteousness I will see your face;
when I awake, I will be satisfied with seeing your likeness.

—PSALM 17:13–15

❧ GREAT PEACE

Rulers persecute me without cause,
but my heart trembles at your word.
I rejoice in your promise like one who finds great spoil.
I hate and abhor falsehood but I love your law.
Seven times a day I praise you for your righteous laws.
Great peace have they who love your law,
and nothing can make them stumble.
I wait for your salvation, O LORD,
and I follow your commands.
I obey your statutes, for I love them greatly.
I obey your precepts and your statutes,
for all my ways are known to you.

—PSALM 119:161–168

WISE SON, DISGRACEFUL SON

The proverbs of Solomon:
A wise son brings joy to his father,
but a foolish son grief to his mother.
Ill-gotten treasures are of no value,
but righteousness delivers from death.
The LORD does not let the righteous go hungry
but he thwarts the craving of the wicked.
Lazy hands make a man poor,
but diligent hands bring wealth.
He who gathers crops in summer is a wise son,
but he who sleeps during harvest is a disgraceful son.

—PROVERBS 10:1–5

❧ YOUR WORDS GIVE LIGHT

Your statutes are wonderful;
therefore I obey them.
The unfolding of your words gives light;
it gives understanding to the simple.
I open my mouth and pant,
longing for your commands.
Turn to me and have mercy on me,
as you always do to those who love your name.
Direct my footsteps according to your word;
let no sin rule over me.
Redeem me from the oppression of men,
that I may obey your precepts.
Make your face shine upon your servant
and teach me your decrees.
Streams of tears flow from my eyes,
for your law is not obeyed.

—PSALM 119:129–136

O My Son

The sayings of King Lemuel—
an oracle his mother taught him:
"O my son, O son of my womb, O son of my vows,
do not spend your strength on women,
your vigor on those who ruin kings.
"It is not for kings, O Lemuel—
not for kings to drink wine,
not for rulers to crave beer,
lest they drink and forget what the law decrees,
and deprive all the oppressed of their rights.
Give beer to those who are perishing,
wine to those who are in anguish;
let them drink and forget their poverty
and remember their misery no more.

—PROVERBS 31:1–7

❧ A TREE OF LIFE

The eyes of the LORD are everywhere,
keeping watch on the wicked and the good.
The tongue that brings healing is a tree of life,
but a deceitful tongue crushes the spirit.
The house of the righteous contains great treasure,
but the income of the wicked brings them trouble.
A hot-tempered man stirs up dissension,
but a patient man calms a quarrel.
The way of the sluggard is blocked with thorns,
but the path of the upright is a highway.

—PROVERBS 15:3, 4, 6, 18, 19

DECEMBER 2

✤ LET US DISCERN FOR OURSELVES

"Hear my words, you wise men;
listen to me, you men of learning.
For the ear tests words
as the tongue tastes food.
Let us discern for ourselves what is right;
let us learn together what is good.

—JOB 34:2–4

In God I Trust

When I am afraid,
I will trust in you.
In God, whose word I praise,
in God I trust; I will not be afraid.
What can mortal man do to me?
All day long they twist my words;
they are always plotting to harm me.
They conspire, they lurk,
they watch my steps,
eager to take my life.

—Psalm 56:3–6

❧ WHY SHOULD ANY LIVING MAN COMPLAIN?

Who can speak and have it happen
if the Lord has not decreed it?
Is it not from the mouth of the Most High
that both calamities and good things come?
Why should any living man complain
when punished for his sins?

—LAMENTATIONS 3:37–39

❧ PRAISE HIM

Praise the LORD.
Praise the LORD from the heavens,
praise him in the heights above.
Praise him, all his angels,
praise him, all his heavenly hosts.
Praise him, sun and moon,
praise him, all you shining stars.
Praise him, you highest heavens
and you waters above the skies.
Let them praise the name of the LORD,
for he commanded and they were created.
He set them in place for ever and ever;
he gave a decree that will never pass away.

—PSALM 148:1–6

BE HAPPY, YOUNG MAN

Be happy, young man, while you are young,
and let your heart give you joy in the days of your youth.
Follow the ways of your heart
and whatever your eyes see,
but know that for all these things
God will bring you to judgment.

—ECCLESIASTES 11:9

✒ YOUR WORD

How can a young man keep his way pure?
By living according to your word.
I seek you with all my heart;
do not let me stray from your commands.
I have hidden your word in my heart
that I might not sin against you.

—PSALM 119:9–11

❧ KEEP YOUR FATHER'S COMMANDS

My son, keep your father's commands
and do not forsake your mother's teaching.
Bind them upon your heart forever;
fasten them around your neck.
When you walk, they will guide you;
when you sleep, they will watch over you;
when you awake, they will speak to you.

—PROVERBS 6:20–22

❧ WHO MAY ASCEND?

Who may ascend the hill of the LORD?
Who may stand in his holy place?
He who has clean hands and a pure heart,
who does not lift up his soul to an idol
or swear by what is false.
He will receive blessing from the LORD
and vindication from God his Savior.
Such is the generation of those who seek him,
who seek your face, O God of Jacob.

—PSALM 24:3–6

❧ EVERY WORD OF GOD

"Every word of God is flawless;
he is a shield to those who take refuge in him.
Do not add to his words,
or he will rebuke you and prove you a liar.

—PROVERBS 30:5–6

❧ You Have Taught Me

But as for me, I will always have hope;
I will praise you more and more.
My mouth will tell of your righteousness,
of your salvation all day long,
though I know not its measure.
I will come and proclaim your mighty acts,
O Sovereign LORD;
I will proclaim your righteousness, yours alone.
Since my youth, O God, you have taught me,
and to this day I declare your marvelous deeds.
Even when I am old and gray,
do not forsake me, O God,
till I declare your power to the next generation,
your might to all who are to come.

—PSALM 71:14–18

TAKE REFUGE IN THE LORD

It is better to take refuge in the LORD
than to trust in man.
It is better to take refuge in the LORD
than to trust in princes.

—PSALM 118:8–9

❧ THE MOST IGNORANT
OF MEN

"I am the most ignorant of men;
I do not have a man's understanding.
I have not learned wisdom,
nor have I knowledge of the Holy One.
Who has gone up to heaven and come down?
Who has gathered up the wind
in the hollow of his hands?

—PROVERBS 30:2–4

I WILL ESTABLISH YOUR THRONE FOREVER

I will sing of the LORD'S great love forever;
with my mouth I will make your faithfulness
known through all generations.
I will declare that your love stands firm forever,
that you established your faithfulness in heaven itself.
You said, "I have made a covenant with my chosen one,
I have sworn to David my servant,
'I will establish your line forever
and make your throne firm through all generations.'"

—PSALM 89:1–4

❦ THE LORD SEARCHES THE SPIRIT OF A MAN

A wise king winnows out the wicked;
he drives the threshing wheel over them.
The lamp of the LORD searches the spirit of a man;
it searches out his inmost being.
Love and faithfulness keep a king safe;
through love his throne is made secure.
The glory of young men is their strength,
gray hair the splendor of the old.

—PROVERBS 20:26–29

DECEMBER 16

❧ THE FAITHFUL HAVE VANISHED

Help, LORD, for the godly are no more;
the faithful have vanished from among men.
Everyone lies to his neighbor;
their flattering lips speak with deception.

—PSALM 12:1–2

❧ Even in Your Thoughts

Do not revile the king even in your thoughts,
or curse the rich in your bedroom,
because a bird of the air may carry your words,
and a bird on the wing may report what you say.

—ECCLESIASTES 10:20

❧ FAITHFULNESS AND RIGHTEOUSNESS

Love and faithfulness meet together;
righteousness and peace kiss each other.
Faithfulness springs forth from the earth,
and righteousness looks down from heaven.
The LORD will indeed give what is good,
and our land will yield its harvest.
Righteousness goes before him
and prepares the way for his steps.

—PSALM 85:10–13

❧ WHOEVER FINDS ME FINDS LIFE

"Now then, my sons, listen to me;
blessed are those who keep my ways.
Listen to my instruction and be wise;
do not ignore it.
Blessed is the man who listens to me,
watching daily at my doors,
waiting at my doorway.
For whoever finds me finds life
and receives favor from the LORD.
But whoever fails to find me harms himself;
all who hate me love death."

—PROVERBS 8:32–36

TASTE AND SEE

The angel of the LORD
encamps around those who fear him,
and he delivers them.
Taste and see that the LORD is good;
blessed is the man who takes refuge in him.
Fear the LORD, you his saints,
for those who fear him lack nothing.
The lions may grow weak and hungry,
but those who seek the LORD lack no good thing.
Come, my children, listen to me;
I will teach you the fear of the LORD.
Whoever of you loves life
and desires to see many good days,
keep your tongue from evil
and your lips from speaking lies.
Turn from evil and do good;
seek peace and pursue it.

—PSALM 34:7–14

❧ REJOICING COMES IN THE MORNING

Sing to the LORD, you saints of his;
praise his holy name.
For his anger lasts only a moment,
but his favor lasts a lifetime;
weeping may remain for a night,
but rejoicing comes in the morning.

—PSALM 30:4–5

THE ABUNDANCE OF A RICH MAN

Whoever loves money never has money enough;
whoever loves wealth is never satisfied with his income.
This too is meaningless.
As goods increase,
so do those who consume them.
And what benefit are they to the owner
except to feast his eyes on them?
The sleep of a laborer is sweet,
whether he eats little or much,
but the abundance of a rich man
permits him no sleep.

—ECCLESIASTES 5:10–12

❧ CHILDREN A REWARD FROM HIM

Sons are a heritage from the LORD,
children a reward from him.
Like arrows in the hands of a warrior
are sons born in one's youth.
Blessed is the man
whose quiver is full of them.
They will not be put to shame
when they contend with their enemies in the gate.

—PSALM 127:3–5

❧ IT IS GOOD TO BE NEAR GOD

Those who are far from you will perish;
you destroy all who are unfaithful to you.
But as for me, it is good to be near God.
I have made the Sovereign LORD my refuge;
I will tell of all your deeds.

—PSALM 73:27–28

❧ AN OATH TO DAVID

The LORD swore an oath to David,
a sure oath that he will not revoke:
"One of your own descendants
I will place on your throne—
if your sons keep my covenant
and the statutes I teach them,
then their sons will sit
on your throne for ever and ever."

—PSALM 132:11–12

A PRUDENT WIFE IS FROM THE LORD

A foolish son is his father's ruin,
and a quarrelsome wife is like a constant dripping.
Houses and wealth are inherited from parents,
but a prudent wife is from the LORD.

—PROVERBS 19:13–14

❧ LIKE THE MIGHTY MOUNTAINS

Your love, O LORD, reaches to the heavens,
your faithfulness to the skies.
Your righteousness is like the mighty mountains,
your justice like the great deep.
O LORD, you preserve both man and beast.
How priceless is your unfailing love!
Both high and low among men
find refuge in the shadow of your wings.
They feast on the abundance of your house;
you give them drink from your river of delights.
For with you is the fountain of life;
in your light we see light.

—PSALM 36:5–9

❧ THE WORDS OF THE LORD ARE FLAWLESS

*"Because of the oppression of the weak
and the groaning of the needy,
I will now arise," says the LORD.
"I will protect them from those who malign them."
And the words of the LORD are flawless,
like silver refined in a furnace of clay,
purified seven times.*

—PSALM 12:5–6

❧ JOB

The LORD blessed the latter part
of Job's life more than the first.
He had fourteen thousand sheep, six thousand camels,
a thousand yoke of oxen and a thousand donkeys.
And he also had seven sons and three daughters.
The first daughter he named Jemimah,
the second Keziah
and the third Keren-Happuch.
Nowhere in all the land were there found women
as beautiful as Job's daughters,
and their father granted them an inheritance
along with their brothers.
After this, Job lived a hundred and forty years;
he saw his children and their children
to the fourth generation.

—JOB 42:12–16

BE GLAD ALL OUR DAYS

Relent, O LORD! How long will it be?
Have compassion on your servants.
Satisfy us in the morning with your unfailing love,
that we may sing for joy and be glad all our days.
Make us glad for as many days as you have afflicted us,
for as many years as we have seen trouble.
May your deeds be shown to your servants,
your splendor to their children.
May the favor of the Lord our God rest upon us;
establish the work of our hands for us—
yes, establish the work of our hands.

—PSALM 90:13–17

THE WHOLE DUTY OF MAN

Now all has been heard;
here is the conclusion of the matter:
Fear God and keep his commandments,
for this is the whole duty of man.
For God will bring every deed into judgment,
including every hidden thing,
whether it is good or evil.

—ECCLESIASTES 12:13–14

EPILOGUE

"Behold, I am coming soon!
My reward is with me,
and I will give to everyone
according to what he has done.
I am the Alpha and the Omega,
the First and the Last,
the Beginning and the End.
Blessed are those who wash their robes,
that they may have the right to the tree of life
and may go through the gates into the city.
Outside are the dogs, those who practice magic arts,
the sexually immoral, the murderers, the idolaters
and everyone who loves and practices falsehood.
I, Jesus, have sent my angel
to give you this testimony for the churches.
I am the Root and the Offspring of David,
and the bright Morning Star."

—FROM REVELATION 22:12–16

SUBJECT INDEX

A

ABUNDANCE
June 25: *Ps. 65:8–13*

ADULTERY
January 25: *Prov. 5:1–6*
January 30: *Prov. 2:12–22*
May 21: *Prov. 7:6–9*
June 30: *Prov. 30:20*
September 4: *Prov. 6:30–35*
October 3: *Prov. 23:26–28*
November 12: *Prov. 7:1–5*

ANGER
July 7: *Prov. 22:24–25*

B

BETRAYAL
July 27: *Ps. 55:20–21*
August 12: *Job 6:14–17*
November 24: *Eccl. 5:4–7*

C

CONFESSION
May 15: *Ps. 38:17–20*

CRAFTINESS
September 25: *Prov. 20:14*

CREATION
January 2: *Ps. 139:13–16*
April 3: *Job 38:1–7*

D

DESPAIR
January 18: *Ps. 42:5–7*
February 16: *Ps. 42:8–11*
March 15: *Eccl. 2:10–11*
March 26: *Ps. 22:6–8*
July 9: *Job 30:20–23*
August 24: *Ps. 88:9–13*
September 2: *Lam. 2:14–16*
September 12: *Lam. 2:11–13*

DILIGENCE
August 25: *Prov. 12:11*

DISCIPLINE
May 12: *Prov. 3:11–12*
May 17: *Prov. 23:13–14*
May 23: *Prov. 4:20–27*
October 10: *Prov. 5:11–14*
November 5: *Prov. 29:15,17*

DIVINE JUSTICE
August 5: *Eccl. 3:16–17*

DIVINE MYSTERY
May 16: *Prov. 30:18–19*
June 8: *Job 38::34–38*
July 14: *Job 7:17–21*

DRUNK, THE
June 16: *Prov. 23:19–21*
November 25: *Prov. 23:29–35*

E

ENVY
June 5: *Ps. 73:2–14*

ETERNITY
June 1: *Eccl. 3:9–11*

EVILDOERS
February 21: *Prov. 24:15–20*
June 11: *Ps. 140:1–5*
June 17: *Ps. 5:4–6*
July 3: *Ps. 64:1–6*
July 6: *Ps. 10:2–5*
July 17: *Ps. 94:20–23*
September 29: *Prov. 26:23–25*
November 9: *Ps. 55:9–11*
November 20: *Prov. 1:10–16*

F

FAITH
February 28: *Ps. 91:9–13*
March 25: *Job 37:14, 19–24*
April 10: *Job 19:23–27*

Man's Sinful Nature *(cont'd.)*
October 26: *Eccl. 8:8*

MARRIAGE
May 7: *Prov. 5:15–20*

MERCY
May 22: *Ps. 123:1–4*
May 25: *Ps. 130:1–6*
June 3: *Ps. 78:32–39*
July 31: *Ps. 73:21–26*
August 23: *Prov. 14:20, 21, 31*

MORTALITY
January 13: *Job 14:1–6*
January 26: *Ps. 90:3–6*
March 13: *Ps. 39:4–6*
March 27: *Ps. 90:7–10*
June 13: *Job 7:6–10*
September 23: *Job 9:25–26*
October 15: *Ps. 49:10–12*

N

NOSTALGIA
August 20: *Eccl. 7:10*

O

OBEDIENCE
February 2: *Ps. 119:9–19*
August 3: *Ps. 119:65–72*
November 29: *Ps. 119:129–136*
December 8: *Prov. 6:20–22*
December 31: *Eccl. 12:13–14*

OLD AGE
May 5: *Eccl. 12:1–5*

P

PATIENCE
April 7: *Ps. 37:5–7*
September 27: *Prov. 19:2*

PRAISE
January 16: *Ps. 89:5–8*
January 19: *Ps. 148:7–13*
February 12: *Ps. 89:9–18*
February 14: *Ps. 30:8–12*
March 10: *Ps. 59:14–17*
April 5: *Ps. 86:11–13*
April 9: *Ps. 118:22–24*
April 19: *Ps. 66:1–4*
April 28: *Ps. 48:1–3*

May 27: *Ps. 114:3–8*
June 19: *Ps. 98:7–9*
July 15: *Ps. 33:1–5*
July 18: *Ps. 67:3–7*
August 11: *Ps. 108:1–5*
August 21: *Ps. 101:1–4*
September 16: *Ps.116:15–16*
November 2: *Ps. 84:10–12*
November 4: *Ps. 115:16–18*
November 19: *Ps. 96:10–13*
December 5: *Ps. 148:1–6*
December 11: *Ps. 71:14–18*
December 21: *Ps. 30:4–5*

PRAYER
February 7: *Ps. 51:10–13*
February 15: *Prov. 30:7–9*
February 18: *Ps. 80:4–8*
February 26: *Ps. 17:1–3*
February 29: *Ps. 28:1–2*
March 29: *Ps. 7:7–9*
April 24: *Ps. 41:4*
April 26: *Ps. 63:1*
May 3: *Ps. 12:7–8*
May 19: *Ps. 25:16–21*
June 9: *Ps. 67:1–2*
July 22: *Ps. 88:1–5*
August 9: *Ps. 31:9–10*
August 27: *Ps. 5:1–3*
September 19: *Ps. 55:1–3*
September 26: *Ps. 27:10–14*
November 26: *Ps. 17:13–15*
December 7: *Ps. 119:9–11*
December 16: *Ps. 12:1–2*
December 30: *Ps. 90:13–17*

PRIDE
March 17: *Ps. 36:1–2*
May 28: *Prov. 16:17, 18, 25*
September 20: *Prov. 30:29–31*

PRUDENCE
January 31:*Prov. 1:1–6*

R

REBELLION
January 23: *Ps. 2:1–4*

REPENTANCE
March 4: *Lam. 3:40–45*
March 6: *Ps. 32:1–5*

RIGHTEOUSNESS
January 3: *Job 1:6–8*
January 4: *Ps. 1:1–3*